D0771208

Madeleine Albright

The People to Know Series

Madeleine Albright
First Woman Secretary of State
0-7660-1143-7

Neil Armstrong
The First Man on the Moon
0-89490-828-6

Isaac Asimov
Master of Science Fiction
0-7660-1031-7

Robert Ballard
Oceanographer Who Discovered the Titanic
0-7660-1147-X

Willa Cather
Writer of the Prairie
0-89490-980-0

Bill Clinton
United States President
0-89490-437-X

Hillary Rodham Clinton
Activist First Lady
0-89490-583-X

Bill Cosby
Actor and Comedian
0-89490-548-1

Walt Disney
Creator of Mickey Mouse
0-89490-694-1

Bob Dole
Legendary Senator
0-89490-825-1

Marian Wright Edelman
Fighting for Children's Rights
0-89490-623-2

Bill Gates
Billionaire Computer Genius
0-89490-824-3

Jane Goodall
Protector of Chimpanzees
0-89490-827-8

Al Gore
Leader for the New Millennium
0-7660-1232-8

Tipper Gore
Activist, Author, Photographer
0-7660-1142-9

Ernest Hemingway
Writer and Adventurer
0-89490-979-7

Ron Howard
Child Star & Hollywood Director
0-89490-981-9

John F. Kennedy
President of the New Frontier
0-89490-693-3

Stephen King
King of Thrillers and Horror
0-7660-1233-6

John Lennon
The Beatles and Beyond
0-89490-702-6

Maya Lin
Architect and Artist
0-89490-499-X

Jack London
A Writer's Adventurous Life
0-7660-1144-5

Barbara McClintock
Nobel Prize Geneticist
0-89490-983-5

Rosie O'Donnell
Talk Show Host and Comedian
0-7660-1148-8

Christopher Reeve
Hollywood's Man of Courage
0-7660-1149-6

Ann Richards
Politician, Feminist, Survivor
0-89490-497-3

Sally Ride
First American Woman in Space
0-89490-829-4

Will Rogers
Cowboy Philosopher
0-89490-695-X

Franklin D. Roosevelt
The Four-Term President
0-89490-696-8

Steven Spielberg
Hollywood Filmmaker
0-89490-697-6

John Steinbeck
America's Author
0-7660-1150-X

Martha Stewart
Successful Businesswoman
0-89490-984-3

Amy Tan
Author of The Joy Luck Club
0-89490-699-2

Alice Walker
Author of The Color Purple
0-89490-620-8

Simon Wiesenthal
Tracking Down Nazi Criminals
0-89490-830-8

Frank Lloyd Wright
Visionary Architect
0-7660-1032-5

People to Know

Madeleine Albright

First Woman Secretary of State

Barbara Kramer

E

Enslow Publishers, Inc.

40 Industrial Road
Box 398
Berkeley Heights, NJ 07922
USA

PO Box 38
Aldershot
Hants GU12 6BP
UK

http://www.enslow.com

Library of Congress Cataloging-in-Publication Data

Kramer, Barbara.
Madeleine Albright : first woman Secretary of State / Barbara Kramer.
p. cm. — (People to know)
Includes bibliographical references (p.) and index.
Summary: Describes the personal life and political career of Madeleine Albright, the first woman to become Secretary of State.
ISBN 0-7660-1143-7
1. Albright, Madeleine Korbel Juvenile literature. 2. Women cabinet officers—United States Biography Juvenile literature. 3. Cabinet officers—United States Biography Juvenile literature. 4. United Nations—Officials and employees Biography Juvenile literature. 5. Ambassadors—United States Biography Juvenile literature. [1. Albright, Madeleine Korbel. 2. Cabinet officers. 3. Ambassadors. 4. Women Biography.] I. Title. II. Series.
E840.8.A37K73 2000
327.73'092—dc21
[B] 99-21294
CIP

Printed in the United States of America

10 9 8 7 6 5 4 3 2 1

To Our Readers:
All Internet addresses in this book were active and appropriate when we went to press. Any comments or suggestions can be sent by e-mail to Comments@enslow.com or to the address on the back cover.

Illustration Credits: AP/Wide World Photos, pp. 64, 70; Courtesy of Wellesley College Archives, p. 22; Express Newspapers/C601/Archive Photos, p. 86; Georgetown University, pp. 37, 46; Reuters/Danilo Krstanovic/Archive Photos, p. 59; Reuters/Jeff Christensen/Archive Photos, p. 42; Reuters/Michael Boddy/Archive Photos, p. 56; Reuters/Mike Segar/Archive Photos, p. 95; Reuters/Mike Theiler/Archive Photos, p. 100; Reuters/Pavel Horejsi/Archive Photos, p. 82; Reuters/Peter Morgan/Archive Photos, p. 51; Reuters/Rick Wilking/Archive Photos, p. 9; Reuters/Win McNamee/Archive Photos, p. 73; Sygma, pp. 16, 25, 30, 76; United States Department of State, p. 6.

Cover Illustration: United States Department of State

Contents

Secretary of State Madeleine K. Albright

1

Telling It Like It Is

On a cold winter day in Washington, D.C., a small group gathered in the Oval Office at the White House. It was January 23, 1997, and Madeleine Korbel Albright was being sworn in as secretary of state. At fifty-nine years old, she was about to become the highest-ranking woman in government in the history of the United States.

The secretary of state is the president's chief advisor on foreign policy and, as such, travels widely to meet with the leaders of other countries. The secretary also heads the State Department, which includes the ambassadors in United States embassies all over the world. There have been some important people in this position, beginning with Thomas Jefferson, the first secretary of state. But people predicted that Albright would not be like any other secretary of state. It is true that she was the first woman to hold that position, but their predictions were based on something more: People were talking about her style.

For the previous four years, Albright had been the United States ambassador to the United Nations. She traveled throughout the world to discuss foreign policy issues. Albright is fluent in the Czech and French languages. She also has good speaking and reading abilities in Russian and Polish. The leaders of other countries like the fact that she talks with them in their own languages.

On the other hand, Albright is outspoken. That is unusual for diplomats. People who work in forcign relations are known for their diplomacy. That means that they choose their words carefully. They try not to say anything that might offend another person or country. Albright is known for saying exactly what is on her mind.

One example was when Albright was hosting a party for the new U.S. ambassador to Italy. It was about a month after she began her work at the United Nations. She started to give a toast, but her guests were not paying attention. After asking them to quiet down several times, she said, "I've had it with you guys. Cut the crap and behave yourselves."[1]

"I tell it like it is," Albright likes to say.[2] Although some people criticize her for that bluntness, others like her because of it.

Albright does give clues to what she is thinking. The pins, or brooches, that she wears on her suit jackets often show what is on her mind. “Everyone will just have to read my pins,” she says.[3] She likes to wear a brooch that fits the occasion. Since she collects them, she has a great variety from which to choose.

She has a brooch in the shape of a hot-air balloon, which she wears when she is happy. Her bumblebee pin reminds her of boxer Muhammed Ali. His motto is “Float like a butterfly, sting like a bee.”[4] Some say that could also be Albright’s motto.

For the swearing-in ceremony, Albright had a sparkly red, white, and blue brooch in the shape of an eagle pinned to her navy blue suit. The bald eagle is

President Bill Clinton and Albright’s daughters watch as new Secretary of State Madeleine Albright is sworn in by Vice President Al Gore, Jr.

the national bird of the United States. When Albright found out that she was to become secretary of state, she had the brooch specially made for the occasion. It showed how proud she was to be appointed to that office.

Becoming secretary of state was something Albright had never imagined would happen. It seemed out of her reach, partly because she had not been born in the United States. She was born in Prague, Czechoslovakia (now the Czech Republic), on May 15, 1937. Her father, Josef Korbel, was a foreign diplomat in Czechoslovakia and a strong believer in democracy. In 1948, when the Communist Party seized control of the Czech government, Korbel sought refuge for himself and his family in the United States. Albright was then eleven years old.

Now, as secretary of state, Albright would represent the country that had welcomed her family so many years before. She was clearly happy about that. "I never even thought about the possibility of being secretary of state before," she said, "because who would have ever thought that a girl who arrived from Czechoslovakia at age eleven could become secretary of state of the most powerful country in the world."[5]

On the other hand, some people said that secretary of state was a job that Albright had been training for most of her life. Her interest in foreign relations started when she was very young. Some of her ideas about foreign policy were influenced by events that happened when she was too young to understand them.

"A Born Leader"

Madeleine Albright was named Marie Jana Korbel when she was born in 1937. Her grandmother gave her the nickname "Madlenka," which would later be changed to Madeleine. Although she was born in Czechoslovakia, Madeleine did not live there long. About the time that she was born, her father was appointed to serve in the Czechoslovak Embassy in Yugoslavia. Josef Korbel, his wife, Mandula (called Anna), and their infant daughter moved to the embassy in Belgrade.

The family had a comfortable life in Belgrade. Korbel was well respected and he and his wife made many friends. But back home in Czechoslovakia, there were already signs of troubles ahead. The

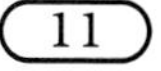

country was located on the southern border of Germany, where Adolf Hitler was in power.

Hitler had become the leader of a political group called the National Socialist German Workers' Party, better known as the Nazis. He had a plan to make Germany strong again after its defeat in World War I. The German people liked what he had to say. He quickly rose to power, becoming chancellor of Germany on January 30, 1933. But Hitler wanted to build an empire. On March 12, 1938, his Nazi troops marched into Austria and easily took control. Then Hitler turned to Czechoslovakia. He demanded that a portion of that country be surrendered to Germany.

For the next six months, leaders from European nations led by Great Britain and France considered Hitler's request. It was less than twenty years since the end of World War I. European leaders seemed willing to do whatever it took to avoid another war. On September 30, 1938, they signed an agreement known as the Munich Pact.

The Munich Pact gave Germany control of about one third of Czechoslovakia. The next day, Nazi troops moved into that country. Three months later, Josef Korbel was recalled from his position in Yugoslavia. He and his wife and daughter returned to Prague.

Madeleine was too young to understand how the Munich Pact would affect their lives. But it would later play a part in her foreign policy decisions. The Munich Pact seriously weakened Czechoslovakia. It gave Hitler a foothold in a country that he wanted to conquer. His Nazi troops soon moved deeper into Czechoslovakia. On the morning of March 15, 1939, they entered the city of Prague. By that evening, German troops controlled the city.

Hitler believed that to have a great empire, he had to get rid of the people he considered undesirable. The biggest such group was the Jews. Other groups were also targeted, including handicapped people, homosexuals, criminals, gypsies, and people who opposed the Nazi Party. Certainly Josef Korbel and his family had reason to fear Hitler, for they were Jewish. However, a more immediate danger for them came from Korbel's position in the Czech government and his strong beliefs in democracy. His name was on a list of people who were to be arrested by the Gestapo, the Nazi secret police.

Madeleine was left with relatives while Josef Korbel looked for a way to get his family out of the country to safety. In the meantime, Josef and Anna Korbel could not go home, where the Nazis would surely find them. Instead, during the day, they roamed the streets of Prague. Each night they stayed with a different friend. "It was mostly in the night that the Gestapo arrested people," Anna Korbel later wrote.[1]

By bribing corrupt officials, Josef Korbel was able to get fake diplomatic papers that said that he, his wife, and their child had permission to leave the country. Ten days after the Nazi invasion, they were on a train headed for Belgrade. All they took with them were two small suitcases, which they hurriedly packed. From there, they traveled to Greece. Then they made their way to England, settling in London.

Edvard Benes, the president of Czechoslovakia, had set up a government-in-exile there.

Josef Korbel was the youngest of three children. His brother, Jan, had already escaped from Czechoslovakia with his family, and they were living in London. Josef Korbel and his family moved into an apartment house in London. In July, Josef Korbel's sister was able to get one of her daughters, eleven-year-old Dagmar Simova, on a train out of Czechoslovakia.

Soon after that, Nazi troops succeeded in sealing off the border of Czechoslovakia. No one was allowed into or out of the country. Other relatives, including Madeleine's three living grandparents and Simova's parents and her older sister, were left behind in Czechoslovakia.

Madeleine was not yet two years old. She was too young to later remember anything about their escape from Czechoslovakia. Her earliest childhood memories are of World War II.

On September 3, 1939, Great Britain and France declared war on Germany. London was the site of heavy bombing, occurring mainly under the cover of darkness. Madeleine spent many nights sleeping on bunk beds in air-raid shelters while German war planes flew overhead. She remembers what it was like to come out of the shelters in the morning and see how the bombs had damaged the city.

Eventually, Josef and Jan Korbel moved their families outside London into a house, which they shared. Later, Madeleine's family moved to a home of their own in a London suburb called Walton-on-Thames. At that time, a type of steel table had just been invented that was supposed to protect people from bombs. "They said if your house was bombed and you were under the table, you would survive," Albright later explained.[2] When the bombing started, they crawled under the table. They sometimes slept there, too, on a small mattress.

Josef Korbel was head of the information department of the Czech government-in-exile in London. He gave reports on the radio that were broadcast in Czechoslovakia through the British Broadcasting Corporation (BBC). Getting news from Czechoslovakia was hard. There were reports of mass executions of Jews taking place in German concentration camps, but the Czech people living in London did not want to believe them.[3] Later, as the reports became more detailed, people knew that they were true.

In spite of the war, Madeleine enjoyed typical childhood experiences. She attended school, where she learned to speak English. She spent her free time riding her bicycle or playing field hockey in an empty lot near their home.

Josef and Jan Korbel shared the expenses of sending Dagmar Simova to a boarding school for girls. Simova spent her vacations with her uncles and their families. She sometimes baby-sat for Madeleine and Madeleine's sister, Katherine (Kathy), who was born in October 1942. Simova said that even then Madeleine showed signs of the adult she would become. "Madeleine was a very bright child, very bossy," Simova later said.[4] She went on to describe her cousin as "a born leader."[5]

The war ended in 1945, and Josef Korbel returned to Prague. He later sent for his family. Anna Korbel, her two daughters, and Dagmar Simova made the trip home in a plane that had been used to carry bombs during the war. Madeleine was then eight years old.

Madeleine's parents learned that her grandparents had died in concentration camps during the war, but they did not share all the details about those deaths with Madeleine. She was told only that her grandparents had died during the war. They also chose not to tell Madeleine about her Jewish heritage. While the Korbels were in England, they had

An eight-year-old Madeleine in London in 1945. After World War II ended, she and her family returned to Prague.

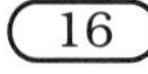

converted to Catholicism. Madeleine was baptized as a Catholic and grew up as a member of that faith.

The Korbels lived in Prague for about three months. Then Josef Korbel was named Czech ambassador to Yugoslavia, and they moved to Belgrade.

Yugoslavia was now under Communist control. Josef Korbel's old friends from that country no longer trusted him because of his belief in democracy. Korbel did not appear to trust them either. He would not allow Madeleine to attend school because he did not want her to be influenced by Communists. She was tutored at home for a while and later sent to a boarding school in Switzerland. It was there that her name was changed to Madeleine.

The language spoken at the Swiss school was French, and the teachers were strict. Madeleine quickly learned to speak French, recalling later that she either had to speak the language or she would not get to eat. By the time she was ten years old, she could already speak three languages—Czech, English, and French.

Moving from one country to another did not seem to have a bad effect on Madeleine. She made friends easily. "My mother always taught me to be open and friendly with new people," Albright later wrote. "She said I could learn a lot from them, and she was right."[6]

Madeleine spent her school vacations in Belgrade, where she helped her father welcome leaders from other countries. Dressed in a traditional Czech costume, she went with her father to the airport. There she greeted their guests, handing them bouquets of flowers.

Josef Korbel served as ambassador to Yugoslavia until 1948. Then he got a temporary assignment to represent Czechoslovakia on a special United Nations team.

The United Nations was formed after World War II. It is an international organization dedicated to working for world peace. Korbel's job was to help find a peaceful solution to a disagreement between the countries of India and Pakistan.

While he traveled in India and Pakistan, Anna Korbel and their children—they now had a young son, John, as well as two daughters—went first to England and later to the United States. They settled near New York City, where the United Nations had its headquarters. Madeleine attended sixth grade near her home in the town of Great Neck.

In the meantime, Czechoslovakia was the site of a political struggle. Before World War II, the Communist Party was in the minority in Czechoslovakia. After the war, the number of Communists in that country grew and finally took control of the Czech government.

Because Josef Korbel did not support the Communist Party, he was considered an enemy of the Czech government. Instead of returning to Czechoslovakia, he asked for political asylum in the United States, and it was granted. This meant that the United States agreed that Korbel's life would be in danger in Czechoslovakia because of his political beliefs. Therefore, Korbel and his family were allowed to live in this country. They later became United States citizens.

In 1949, Josef Korbel got a job as professor of international relations at the University of Denver. The family headed for Colorado in a green Ford that they bought for the trip.

Madeleine really wanted to become a typical American teen. Although she spoke English, she had a British accent, which she worked hard to lose. She also kept up-to-date on the latest fashions. "I spent a lot of time worrying, trying to make sure that I would fit in," Albright recalled. "I wanted very much to be an American."[7]

She also wanted to please her father, whom she admired. "A great deal of what I did," she said, "I did because I wanted to be like my father."[8] He believed in a good education, and Madeleine worked hard at her studies. Josef Korbel wrote books about foreign affairs and Eastern Europe, and Madeleine wrote school papers on those same topics.

Madeleine liked to ski, play field hockey, and swim. She also learned to play the piano, but her real interest was foreign relations. "In my parents' home we talked about international relations all the time, the way some families talk about sports or other things around the dinner table," she explained.[9]

Wherever she went to school, she set up an international relations club. Because she was the founder of the clubs, she always made herself president. She also won an essay contest that was sponsored by the United Nations.

Josef Korbel's students from the university often

visited in the Korbel home. Madeleine listened while the students talked with her father about foreign relations. By the time Madeleine was in high school, she knew more about international relations than many adults. "I think I was pretty boring in high school," she said. "I was a foreign policy wonk [nerd] even then."[10]

Although Madeleine admired her father, she did not always agree with him. Josef Korbel was strict, old-fashioned, and very formal. In fact, he was so formal that he supposedly wore a topcoat and tie when he learned to ski on Colorado's snowy slopes.[11] It was no surprise that his views sometimes clashed with Madeleine's desire to be a typical American teen.

Albright said that one of her biggest disagreements with her father was over which high school to attend. Her father insisted that she accept a scholarship she was offered from a private girls high school. The school was small, with only sixteen in her graduating class. Albright later admitted that it was the right choice. She said she got a good education there. Also, because they wore uniforms, she did not need to worry so much about fitting in.

Another disagreement she had with her father was about her high school prom. Josef Korbel would not allow her to ride alone with her date in a car. She was finally allowed to go, but her father followed them in his car. After the dance, he picked her up and took her home.

Madeleine's father expected a lot from his daughter. But he also taught her that with hard work she could succeed at whatever she wanted to do.

3

Dr. Albright

By the time Madeleine Korbel graduated from high school in Colorado in 1955, she spoke English without a trace of a foreign accent. She accepted a scholarship to attend Wellesley College in Wellesley, Massachusetts, and headed east.

In the 1950s, young women were taught that their future was to become good wives and mothers. Albright's college friends, who called her "Maddy," said that even then she was different. "She was very driven in a way that was not standard for women of the fifties," one of them recalled.[1]

Albright's father got a reminder of how strong-willed his daughter could be. He bought her a typewriter to take with her to college, but there was one condition. Josef Korbel told his daughter that he

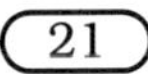

did not want her to use the typewriter to write letters home. He wanted her to write those letters in longhand in Czech.

Madeleine Korbel agreed to that condition, but then her father went one step too far. He marked corrections on her first letters and mailed them back to her. After that, she did not write home anymore. She phoned instead.

Madeleine Korbel was active in politics on campus. The majority of the students were Republicans,

Madeleine Korbel (seated left of the typewriter at the far side of the table) meets with other members of the Wellesley College news staff. As a student, she was interested in journalism and politics.

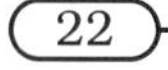

but Korbel, like her father, was a Democrat. She was one of the relatively few students at Wellesley who campaigned for Adlai Stevenson, the Democratic candidate for president in 1956.

She was also interested in journalism, and she wrote articles about politics for the campus newspaper. During the summer of 1957, she worked as an intern at the *Denver Post*. There she met Joseph Patterson Albright, another summer intern who also attended school in the East, Williams College in Williamstown, Massachusetts. Joseph Albright was from a newspaper family. His grandfather had founded the *New York Daily News*. His aunt, Alicia Patterson, was the owner of *Newsday*, based on Long Island, near New York City.

Madeleine Korbel graduated with honors from Wellesley College in 1959, earning a bachelor's degree in political science. Three days later, on June 11, she married Joseph Albright, becoming Madeleine Korbel Albright. Although she had been brought up as a Roman Catholic, Albright converted to her husband's Episcopalian faith.

Soon after their marriage, they moved to Chicago, where Joseph Albright started a job at the *Sun Times*. Madeleine Albright was also interested in working at the newspaper, but her plans were quickly changed. An editor at the newspaper told her that they would not allow a husband and wife to work for the same newspaper. He also said that it would not be right for her to work for a competing newspaper. He said she should find a different kind of work.

Albright admitted that the editor made her angry.

He not only acted as if her career was unimportant, but also called her "Honey." She thought that was insulting. She later said that she was amazed that she did not fight back. "But it was 1960, and I'd been married half a year," she recalled.[2] It was a time when women were not encouraged to have careers of their own.

She did find a job at the *Encyclopedia Britannica*, but she worked there only a short time. Her husband was soon named city editor of *Newsday*, and the couple moved to Long Island.

In 1961, Albright gave birth to twin daughters, Anne and Alice. They were born six weeks premature. Their small size meant that they had to stay in the hospital for special care. To get her mind off worrying so much about her babies, Albright took a Russian language course at Columbia University in New York City.

Two months after their birth, Albright's daughters were finally able to leave the hospital. Albright had her hands full when she took them home. They were still small and needed frequent feedings. She had to get up three times during the night to feed them.

Although Albright was busy with her daughters, she did not feel challenged. "I kind of sat there during the day, feeding them, watching soap operas, and I thought, I didn't go to college to do this," she said.[3] With the help of a full-time housekeeper/baby-sitter, she began working toward a master's degree in political science at Columbia University.

In 1967, the Albrights had another daughter. They named her Katherine, but they usually called her by

Albright holds her twin daughters, Alice and Anne, who were born in 1961.

her nickname, "Katie." The following year, Albright earned her master's degree from Columbia University and a certificate from the university's Russian Institute. She then decided to work for a Ph.D. degree at Columbia. The Ph.D. degree, or doctorate, is the highest award that a student can earn from a university. Those who receive that degree are called doctors.

Albright's education plans hit a snag when her husband accepted a promotion to head *Newsday*'s Washington, D.C., bureau. It meant another move, but Albright was determined not to give up her studies at Columbia University. She made arrangements with her faculty advisor, Zbigniew Brzezinski, to continue working on her Ph.D. long-distance.

To get that degree, she had to write a book-length report known as a dissertation. Albright combined her interests in journalism and Czech history to come up with a topic: the role of the press in Czechoslovakia in 1968.

At that time, Alexander Dubcek was head of the Communist Party in Czechoslovakia. He instituted reforms that included more freedom of the press. This was known as the "thaw" or "Czech spring" of 1968. However, Communists in other countries feared that these reforms would cause the Communist Party to lose power. In August 1968, Communist troops from the Soviet Union, Bulgaria, East Germany, Hungary, and Poland invaded Czechoslovakia. As a result, Dubcek was removed from power and his reforms were overturned.

Albright said that writing her dissertation was the hardest thing she ever did. She spent many hours doing research, which included interviewing people who had been involved with that movement. She needed quiet time to write, so she rose at 4:30 in the morning to work on her dissertation.

However, she was not the type of person who liked to spend a lot of time alone. She needed activities that would give her a chance to be with other people. When her twins were in second grade, she began volunteering at the private school they attended. She served on the board of directors and also began working as a fund-raiser for the school.

Albright had no experience in raising money, but she worked hard and it paid off. "I got the reputation of getting the job done," she recalled.[4]

One of the other volunteers introduced Albright to Edmund Muskie, a Democratic senator from Maine. Muskie was running for the Democratic presidential nomination in the 1972 election campaign. Albright helped with his fund-raising, but not for long because Muskie did not win the nomination.

For the next few years, Albright focused on raising her daughters and writing her dissertation. Some people could not understand why getting a Ph.D. degree was so important to Albright. She was already living a life that many people envied. Her husband was a successful journalist. He came from a wealthy family, which allowed him and his wife and daughters to enjoy a comfortable lifestyle. They lived in a five-bedroom, two-story home in Washington, D.C., and spent their weekends on a 370-acre farm they owned in Virginia. But Albright had never lost her passion for foreign relations.

As a child, she had listened to her parents discuss international affairs at the dinner table. Now she did the same with her daughters. Anne Albright later recalled a time when she asked her parents about an ongoing conflict in the Middle East. They explained exactly what was happening and even drew a map on a napkin to help her understand what they were talking about. Anne said that type of conversation happened often in their home.

Although Albright was busy with her studies, her daughters say she always had time for them. She was there to send them off to school in the morning and to help them with their homework at night. She also shuttled them to their activities, which included ballet classes and guitar lessons. Cooking is not one of Albright's favorite activities, but she did enjoy baking with her daughters during weekends at the farm.

Albright was able to handle her busy schedule because she believed in never wasting a moment. "She even knitted in a movie theater," a reporter later wrote.[5]

In the meantime, Senator Muskie had not forgotten the hard work Albright did for him when he was campaigning for the presidential nomination. He was head of the Senate Foreign Relations Committee, and in 1976 he hired Albright to be his chief legislative assistant.

"I had just received my Ph.D.," Albright told a reporter. "That made it possible for Senator Muskie to introduce me as Dr. Albright, instead of Madeleine Albright, little housewife."[6] She was thirty-nine years old, and this was her first paid political job.

"Shoot, Sit, or Negotiate"

Albright told her daughters that they could call her at work anytime. One time when they called, the receptionist told them that their mother could not come to the phone. The receptionist said that Albright was "on the floor with the Senator."[1]

That meant that Albright was attending a Senate meeting with her boss, Senator Muskie. Her daughters had never heard that phrase before and they did not understand. When Albright returned their call, the first thing they asked was "What were you doing on the floor with Senator Muskie?"[2]

Albright's coworkers liked her determination. "When she said she was going to get something done, she got it done," one of them noted.[3] Albright worked

Albright with Senator Edmund Muskie. In 1976, Muskie hired Albright to be his chief legislative assistant.

for Muskie for two years. Then in 1978, one of her former professors, Zbigniew Brzezinski, offered her a job.

Brzezinski was President Jimmy Carter's National Security Advisor. His job was to advise the president on foreign policy issues. Brzezinski was also in charge of the National Security Council staff, which Albright joined.

The National Security Council staff researches and prepares reports for the president on foreign policy issues. When someone wants to talk to the president about national security, he or she first talks to a member of the staff. Albright's position was a step up from the job she had with Muskie. She received a higher salary and more responsibility.

Two years later, Carter lost his reelection bid for president to Ronald Reagan. President Reagan appointed a new National Security Advisor, who put together his own staff. Albright had to find a new job, and she put her research abilities to good use.

In 1981, she received fellowship grants to work on two research projects. A fellowship is money to be used for a special study. Those who are selected to work on the study are called fellows. Albright became a senior fellow at the Center for Strategic and International Studies in Washington. There she researched Soviet and Eastern European affairs.

Albright also won an international competition to receive a fellowship at the Woodrow Wilson International Center for Scholars at the Smithsonian Institution in Washington. As part of that study, she wrote a book titled *Poland, the Role of the Press in Political Change*, which was published in 1983.

Albright suffered a serious setback in her personal life when her husband told her that he wanted a divorce. She has never forgotten the details of that day. It was January 13, 1982. She and her husband were sitting in the living room of their Washington home. Without warning, he looked at her and said, "This marriage is dead and I'm in love with somebody else."[4]

The divorce settlement left Albright well off financially. She kept their Washington home, their farm in Virginia, and investments that are now worth millions. But she was hurt and angry.[5]

They had been married twenty-three years. Albright says she had no idea that her husband was not happy in their marriage. She did not want a divorce and made that clear to anyone who would listen. At the same time, she was not content to be the ex–Mrs. Albright. She had to be active. She took a few months to decide what she would do next.

Then, in the spring of 1982, she began teaching foreign relations at Georgetown University in Washington, D.C. Albright was able to talk about foreign relations in a way that was easy to understand. That made her a popular teacher with the students.

She made her classes more interesting by getting the students involved. One thing she used was role-playing. She had students take the parts of various government officials in discussions of foreign policy issues. She always made sure that the young women in her classes took the roles of men. It was her way of involving women in foreign relations, a field dominated by men.

Albright was also the director of the Women in Foreign Service Program at the university. She taught the young women in her classes not to be afraid to say what they were thinking. It was a lesson Albright had learned from her own experiences. She recalled attending meetings at the White House when she was on the National Security Council staff. At those meetings, she would think of something she wanted to say. Sometimes she would hesitate because she was not sure that it would fit into the conversation. Then a man would say the same thing she had been thinking, and everyone would think it was a good idea. That taught her to speak up sooner. "There are lots of shy people in the world," she told her students, "and they don't go anywhere."[6]

Some of the other professors at Georgetown were critical of Albright. They thought she was more interested in politics than in academics. Albright admitted that she was different from most of the faculty members. "I wasn't a normal professor," she said. "I had worked in government. I hadn't written nine zillion books."[7]

College professors are expected to write scholarly papers in their field. Albright had done some writing, but not the right kind, according to her critics. "She hasn't written books that are considered pathbreaking," one of them noted.[8]

Albright's critics were definitely right about one thing: She loved politics.[9] During the 1980s, her Washington home became a gathering place for leaders in the Democratic Party. They attended dinners hosted by Albright. The meals, prepared by her housekeeper, were always simple. The food was not important. What was important was the conversation that took place after dinner. That was when Albright and her guests discussed current foreign policy issues.

People have disagreed about how important these meetings were. One reporter wrote: "These were not mere social gatherings, but sessions aimed at laying the groundwork for a Democratic return to power."[10]

Some people said Albright used these meetings for networking. The country had a Republican president and Albright was a Democrat. Presidents usually fill important positions with members of their own political party. As a result, with a Republican president, Albright would not have an important role in foreign policy. That could change if a Democrat were elected president. People said that Albright held these meetings to gain power among Democrats. Her hope was to be appointed to a political position under a Democratic president.

Others have said that Albright never intended for the dinners to be a way to boost her career. They said she hosted the dinners because she enjoyed talking about foreign relations with others like herself.

Albright says that her career plans were not that carefully thought out. "The best things that happened to me are the ones I haven't planned for," she explained. "I'm prepared for them. That's something different."[11]

One thing was clear—more and more people were

seeking Albright's opinions on foreign policy. She became Geraldine Ferraro's advisor on foreign policy during the 1984 presidential election. Walter Mondale, the Democratic candidate for president, had named Ferraro as his running mate. She was the first woman to run for vice president. They lost to Republican Ronald Reagan, who was reelected.

In 1988, Albright took a one-semester leave of absence from Georgetown University to serve as foreign policy advisor to Democratic presidential candidate Michael Dukakis. Albright said that her role in that campaign was to make contacts and to find answers to the questions Dukakis asked. Others said there was more to her job. According to reports, she wrote many of his speeches. She also explained his foreign policy to the press.

Many people thought that Albright did a good job as a foreign policy advisor to Dukakis. One of Albright's coworkers explained why: "She is very balanced in her judgments, open to all kinds of people and listens well."[12]

On the other hand, some people criticized her. They said that she was not intellectual enough. They also said that she was good at networking but did not have the ability to plan strategy. "I'm not that smart," Albright once said. Then she went on to explain the secret of her success: "I work very hard."[13]

Another supporter of Dukakis was Bill Clinton, the governor of Arkansas. Albright met Clinton when he made a trip to Boston to help Dukakis prepare for the presidential debate. Dukakis lost the election to George Bush, but Clinton and Albright kept in touch.

In October 1989, Albright was named president of the Center for National Policy in Washington, D.C. The center is a nonprofit research organization formed to study international issues. In her role as president of the center, Albright conducted meetings on Capitol Hill with members of Congress and leaders from other countries.

Albright also continued to teach at Georgetown University. Her students liked her so much that her senior classes voted her most outstanding teacher in the School of Foreign Service four years in a row, 1988 to 1991. That was a record at the university.

It was challenging for Albright to prepare for her classes on foreign relations because so much was happening in the world. A carefully planned lecture could be changed at the last minute because of events in the morning news.

Albright was especially interested in what was happening in Eastern Europe, where Communist regimes were collapsing. Communist countries were now becoming democratic, and Albright was asked to help with the changes. In January 1990, she traveled to Eastern Europe to give workshops on how democracy works. In Hungary, she talked about how to run a political campaign, including how to finance it. In Czechoslovakia, she helped President Vaclav Havel create an election law. What she did in each country depended on what the leaders of that country wanted. "We only do what they ask for," Albright noted.[14]

While she was in Czechoslovakia, Albright got to talk with some old friends. They were people she had interviewed when she was writing her dissertation for

Albright poses with students from one of her classes at Georgetown University. Her students voted her outstanding teacher in the School of Foreign Service four years in a row.

her Ph.D. from Columbia University. Through the years, she had kept in contact with them. They had worked hard for democracy in their country. Now they were becoming the new leaders in Czechoslovakia. Vaclav Havel made his first trip to the United States about a month later. Albright helped plan his visit and served as his interpreter during his stay.

While Albright enjoyed the changes taking place in Eastern Europe, the news from another part of the world was not as happy. On August 2, 1990, Iraqi troops invaded the neighboring country of Kuwait.

Kuwait, a small Middle Eastern country, is rich in

oil. People in the United States and other countries depend on that oil. Iraq also has large quantities of oil. If Iraq were to gain control of Kuwait's oil, then a large amount of the world's oil supply would be in the hands of the Iraqis. Americans saw this as a serious threat to the United States and world economies.

On August 6, 1990, the United Nations voted for economic sanctions, or penalties, against Iraq. With the sanctions, Iraq could not export its oil or receive any imports, not even necessary items such as food. The sanctions were meant to hurt Iraq's economy and pressure Saddam Hussein, the president of Iraq, to withdraw his troops from Kuwait. These sanctions were further strengthened on August 25, when the United Nations passed another ruling. This resolution authorized the use of force to stop ships of countries attempting to trade with Iraq in spite of the sanctions.

In the meantime, President Bush ordered U.S. troops into Saudi Arabia, which borders Iraq and Kuwait. By stationing troops there, Bush hoped to prevent Iraq from invading other areas. It was also the first step in preparing to force Iraqi troops out of Kuwait if they did not leave voluntarily.

Albright paid close attention to what was happening. In October 1990, she was one of three people invited to meet with a group of congressmen to discuss the situation in Kuwait. Albright said the United States had three choices: "Shoot, sit, or negotiate."[15]

"What You See Is What You Get"

Albright was against going to war with Iraq. She thought it was too risky. She believed that Saddam Hussein had deadly chemical weapons and would use them. She said there was nothing to stop him from "setting off chemicals before we finish him."[1]

One person who agreed with her was Colin Powell, the chairman of the Joint Chiefs of Staff. The Joint Chiefs of Staff is made up of the heads of the U.S. Army, Air Force, Navy, and Marines. The chairman is in charge of all four military branches and reports to the president and the secretary of defense.

Other foreign policy leaders did not agree with Albright. They were convinced that Saddam would not withdraw from Kuwait voluntarily. The United States formed a partnership with about thirty other countries that were prepared to take action against Iraq. President Bush gave Powell the job of coming up with a plan for military action.

On November 29, 1990, the United Nations passed a resolution that cleared the way for these countries to act. They were authorized to use force against Iraq if Saddam's troops did not withdraw from Kuwait. They set January 15, 1991, as the date for withdrawal. When Iraq did not meet that deadline, the Gulf War began.

The United States supplied most of the troops and equipment for the war, with some help from France and Great Britain. Countries such as Saudi Arabia, Germany, and Japan gave financial support. But it was the United States that made the military decisions that led to Iraq's defeat. Colin Powell became a new American hero for his role in planning the military strategy. Albright later said that she had been wrong to oppose that war.

In the meantime, Albright continued teaching at Georgetown University. She was also busy with her work as president of the Center for National Policy. Because of that position, Albright had to remain neutral when Bill Clinton ran for president in 1992. Although she did not officially campaign for Clinton, unofficially she did advise him on foreign policy issues.

People predicted that if Clinton were elected, Albright would surely be in line for an important foreign relations position in his administration. Many thought she would become national security advisor.

Others thought she might be named secretary of state.

Clinton won the election, and as expected, he had a place for Albright on his foreign policy team. On December 22, he nominated her to be U.S. ambassador to the United Nations.

Albright was proud to be nominated. In a press conference to accept that honor, she talked about coming to the United States with her family when she was eleven years old. "As a result of the generous spirit of the American people, our family had the privilege of growing up as free Americans," she said. "You can therefore understand how proud I will be to sit at the United Nations behind the nameplate that says 'United States of America.'"[2]

The Albright nomination still needed the approval of the Senate. It would vote after she appeared before the Senate Foreign Relations Committee for her confirmation hearings. Albright was not sure that some of the senators would like what she had to say at those hearings.

It seems that Albright already knew she would need to be more than ambassador to the United Nations. She would also need to be a salesperson. Some Americans did not have much faith in the power of the United Nations. Albright would have to "sell" the United Nations to the American people and to Congress.

Americans had reason to feel as they did. In the past, the United Nations had struck them as ineffective at times. That had a lot to do with how it is organized. The largest part of the United Nations is

On December 22, 1992, President Bill Clinton nominated Albright to be U.S. ambassador to the United Nations. Albright responded that she would be proud to sit behind the nameplate that read "United States."

the General Assembly. It is made up of one representative from each of the 185 member countries. However, much of the work of the United Nations is done in the Security Council.

The Security Council has fifteen members. Five countries have permanent seats in the Security Council—China, France, Great Britain, the Soviet Union (the seat was taken over by Russia in 1990), and the United States. The other ten members are elected by the General Assembly to serve two-year terms. Each of the permanent members of the Security Council has veto power. By using that veto, individual members sometimes can make the United Nations ineffective. That was where the problem with power in the United Nations lay.

The relationship between two member countries—the United States and the Soviet Union—was one of fear and distrust. That situation, dating back to the end of World War II, was known as the Cold War. Both countries had veto power in the Security Council, and since they seldom agreed, the United Nations often appeared powerless.

That changed in 1989 with the fall of Communism in the Soviet Union. Relations between the Soviet Union and the United States became friendlier. Albright had openly criticized President Bush for not adapting U.S. foreign policy to deal with this change.

Another problem with the United Nations, according to some Republican members of Congress, was the way United Nations funds were being used. Congressmen said that too much money was spent on running the organization. They said it was money that should be going to the people and countries that the United Nations was trying to help.

Each member country is expected to contribute to funding the United Nations, although every country does not pay the same amount. Dues are based on each nation's economy. That means that the United States is expected to pay a large share. When Albright was nominated to be ambassador, the United States was more than a billion dollars behind in its dues. That made some other member countries angry, but Congress would not agree to pay up. Congress was holding out for changes to be made in the way United Nations funds were used and in the proportion of the dues that the United States was required to pay.

Albright planned to talk about these issues at her confirmation hearing. She knew that it might hurt her chances to become ambassador. On the other hand, she was not going to let that keep her from saying what she thought needed to be said. "With me, what you see is what you get," she said. "If the senators on the committee don't like what I have to say, then they don't like it."[3]

In January 1993, Albright appeared before the Senate committee for her confirmation hearing. She talked about the end of the Cold War and what that meant for the United Nations. She also said that it was time for the United States to pay its outstanding dues to the UN.

After Albright's presentation, the senators were allowed to question her. The Democrats questioned her in the morning, and the Republican senators had their chance that afternoon. Members of the press were expecting a battle between Albright and Jesse Helms, the Republican senator from North Carolina who was chairman of the Senate Foreign Relations Committee. Both were used to saying what they thought, and Helms was extremely critical of the United Nations. That battle never happened. Helms listened thoughtfully while Albright spoke. He later noted that her childhood experiences had made her a fighter for human rights and democracy. Those were good qualities for an ambassador in the United Nations.

Other people have also noted Albright's concern for human rights. "When Madeleine sits at the table, she is very often the voice of conscience saying we *should* do this or we *should* do that," one White House insider said.[4]

On January 21, 1993, the Senate unanimously approved Albright's nomination. She became the country's twenty-first ambassador to the United Nations. Albright then moved into the ambassador's official residence, on the thirty-second floor of the Waldorf-Astoria Hotel in New York City. On February 6, she began her work at the United Nations.

President Clinton made Albright's position even more important when he gave it Cabinet-level status, meaning that Albright would attend meetings of the Cabinet—a group of advisors to the president. This was not something new. Presidents are allowed to decide who they want to attend Cabinet meetings. In 1961, President John F. Kennedy had given Adlai Stevenson, his ambassador to the United Nations, Cabinet rank.

Faculty and students at Georgetown University celebrate Albright's appointment as U.S. ambassador to the United Nations. Speaking with Albright is Allan Goodman, who was then a professor and administrator in Georgetown's School of Foreign Service.

Albright was a great admirer of Adlai Stevenson. When she was in college, she had campaigned for him when he ran for president of the United States. Now she was following in his footsteps—an ambassador to the United Nations with Cabinet rank.

In her office at the United Nations, Albright placed a bust of Stevenson on a bookcase where it was clearly visible from her desk. Other decorations in her office included a Harlem Globetrotters jersey and a basketball that had been signed by members of the team.

One of the first things Albright did as ambassador

was to organize regular lunches with the other women in the United Nations. It was a small group, for there were only seven women representatives in the UN at the time.

Albright was living in New York City, but she also spent a lot of time in Washington, D.C., where she attended Cabinet meetings and other top-level foreign policy meetings. As a result, she became a regular flyer on the New York–D.C. shuttle. Sometimes she would just be landing in Washington when she would get a call to fly back for an important UN matter. She would then get on the next plane and head for New York. If planes were grounded because of weather, Albright took the train. If that was not possible, she relied on videoconferences.

Albright admitted that it was not easy trying to be in two places at once. "It's a little hard when you can't remember where you're spending the night," she said. "I do wake up . . . and there is that moment when you don't know where you are."[5]

Some delegates at the United Nations criticized Albright for these trips. They said she did not spend enough time at the UN and did not take her job seriously. They also said that when she was at the United Nations, she spent too much time seeking out television cameras.

Other people did not feel that way. "The people I work with appreciate the fact that I'm plugged into Washington," Albright noted. "I'm in the inner circle. I'm involved in everything."[6]

It was true that Albright did spend more time with the press than other ambassadors in the past. It was part of her role as salesperson for the United Nations. She wanted people to know more about the United Nations and what was happening in foreign policy. She knew that the press was a valuable aid in getting information to the people. She even called CNN, the cable television news channel, "the 16th member of the Security Council."[7]

Another way that Albright kept Americans informed about the work of the United Nations was to travel throughout the country giving speeches about the UN and foreign policy. She was also the first UN ambassador to have her own Web site.

Albright had such a full schedule that people wondered how she had enough energy to get everything done. She said frequent naps helped and noted that she could fall asleep "on anything that moves."[8]

She did have one regret about her busy life: It was hard to find time to spend with her family. Her daughters understood, but they still teased her about it when they had the chance. In April 1993, Albright received an award for being an outstanding mother of the year. When her daughters heard the news, they jokingly asked, "Who voted?"[9]

6

First Year

During her first year as UN ambassador, Albright changed her mind about the role of the United States in foreign policy. Early in her term, Albright had said that the United States should not act alone to settle conflicts in other countries. She urged U.S. foreign policy leaders to work with international groups, such as the United Nations. She later changed that philosophy, saying that the United States needed to be a leader. Sometimes that meant acting alone. The reason she switched viewpoints had a lot to do with events that happened that first year.

When Albright became ambassador, the United Nations was becoming involved in a peacekeeping mission in the African country of Somalia. Thousands of innocent Somali people were being killed in the fighting between rival clans that had begun after a rebel group overthrew the military government in 1991. Others were being driven from their homes. They fled to cities, which quickly became overcrowded with refugees, people who had left their homes to seek safety and now had no place to go. People were starving or dying from disease because there was not enough food and medical supplies.

The Red Cross started a relief effort in Somalia but did not make much progress. Bandits stole the supplies from trucks before they could reach the people who needed them. In December 1992, President Bush had sent United States troops to Somalia to aid in the relief effort.

Some Americans were surprised that Bush sent United States troops into action during his last month in office. But many, including Albright, believed that he did the right thing. The nightly news aired stories about the men, women, and children who were starving in Somalia. Americans were troubled by the misery. Bush saw a need to act quickly, which was something the United Nations could not do.

The United Nations does not have a permanent army. For each peacekeeping mission, member countries send troops and equipment. This takes time to organize. The United States, on the other hand, had soldiers trained and ready to go to Africa.

On December 9, 1992, United States soldiers landed on the eastern shore of Somalia in the city of Mogadishu. It was the first step of a two-step plan. U.S. troops would open roads and protect trucks carrying supplies to the people. The second step of the plan was to gradually turn the operation over to UN forces.

In a statement made on March 12, 1993, Albright said Americans should be proud of the progress made in Somalia. She noted that between December 9, 1992, and February 19, 1993, "seventy thousand tons of food and medical supplies had been delivered . . . to those in need."[1]

That month the Security Council unanimously passed a resolution to send a UN force to replace the United States-led operation in Somalia. Then, just when Americans thought that their soldiers would soon be coming home, the nature of the military mission changed. What had begun as a relief effort

Albright shows her approval after the United Nations Security Council voted to replace U.S. soldiers in Somalia with UN forces.

became an attempt to capture Somali warlords or leaders. General Mohammad Farah Aidid was a particular target.

In August, four American soldiers were killed carrying out this assignment. After those deaths, Americans began to question the United States role in Somalia. Why had the mission changed? They also wondered whether the United States should be in Somalia at all.

Albright answered their questions in an article she wrote for *The New York Times*, published on August 10, 1993. She wrote that there was no chance for peace in Somalia until the warlords were stopped. She blamed Aidid for the deaths of thirty peacekeepers from other countries. She said Aidid was also responsible for killing four journalists, six Somali people working for the United Nations, and the four American soldiers.

Unfortunately, the situation in Somalia got worse. On October 3, 1993, Somali forces ambushed American soldiers in Mogadishu. They shot down three U.S. helicopters and killed eighteen American soldiers. An angry Somali mob dragged the body of one of the helicopter crewmen through the streets of Mogadishu. Spectators along the streets threw rocks and other objects at the body. Others torched American flags and tried to use them to set the body on fire.

News cameras captured all of this, and Americans at home watched it on their television screens. They were shocked by the scene and became even more anxious to bring their servicemen home. According to a survey in *Time* magazine, 79 percent of the American people had approved of having U.S. troops in Somalia in January 1993. By October, that figure had dropped to 36 percent.[2]

It was not clear how the role of the United States in Somalia changed from relief aid to disarming Somali warlords. Some blamed the United Nations. Boutros Boutros-Ghali, an Egyptian diplomat, who was secretary-general of the United Nations, blamed the United States. Others blamed Madeleine Albright. Critics said she was "too tough, too reckless."[3]

The problems in Somalia made Americans less willing to get involved in a similar situation in the Balkans. The former Yugoslavia had been made up of six different republics and had three main ethnic groups—the Serbs, the Croats, and the Muslims. These groups had lived together peaceably under Communist rule. That changed with the fall of communism in Europe in the early 1990s. Four of the republics then declared their independence from Yugoslavia. It meant the end of that country as it had been known. Civil war broke out as the ethnic groups began fighting over territory.

The area that got the most attention in the United States was Bosnia, which declared its independence in 1992. Bosnian Serbs and Bosnian Croats tried to force the Bosnian Muslims out of the area. The Serbs bombed cities where large groups of Muslims lived. They surrounded the cities, keeping food and medical supplies from getting through to the people. They drove Muslims from their homes, killing them or sending them to detention camps.

The situation in Bosnia was a personal one for Albright. It reminded her of an earlier time. It was the same thing that had happened to the Jews in Czechoslovakia when Hitler invaded that country. The United Nations began a relief effort to get supplies to Bosnia, but it did not have enough soldiers to carry out that mission. The United States tried to help by airdropping supplies. Albright thought stronger actions were needed.

In April 1993, Albright sent a memo to President Clinton calling for air strikes against the Serbs. The strikes would target bridges and ports, which were used in shipping weapons to the Serbs. They would also attack tanks and large weapons.

The air strikes would be carried out by the North Atlantic Treaty Organization (NATO), which had been formed in 1949. NATO had sixteen member countries in 1993: the United States, Canada, and fourteen European nations. The primary purpose of this organization is to provide stability among European countries.

Colin Powell, the chairman of the Joint Chiefs of Staff who stayed on under Clinton, was against Albright's plan for air strikes in Bosnia. Albright and Powell had agreed about the Gulf War. This time they were on opposite sides. During foreign policy meetings over the next few months, they often argued about what to do in Bosnia. Newspapers and magazines carried stories about their disagreements.

It was a difficult time for Albright. Many people thought that she had no right to disagree with Powell about a military matter. After all, he had planned the strategy that led to victory in the Gulf War. "It wasn't easy being a civilian woman having a disagreement with the hero of the Western world," Albright later admitted.[4]

At one meeting in particular, Albright became very frustrated with Powell. "What's the point of having this superb military that you're always talking about if we can't use it?" she blurted out.[5]

Powell said that he was shocked that Albright would say such a thing. "American GIs were not toy soldiers to be moved around on some sort of global game board," he later wrote.[6]

Some people said that Powell's criticism was unfair. They noted that Albright cares deeply about American soldiers. She considers the military her partner in foreign policy. As ambassador to the United Nations, she made it a priority to visit U.S. troops stationed at peacekeeping operations all over the world. She knows the danger these Americans face and the sacrifices they make. She experienced the danger firsthand when she visited U.S. soldiers in Mogadishu. For protection, she had to ride in an armored car and wear a flak jacket. A flak jacket is a vest made of steel plates, which protect the body from shrapnel. These plates are padded with fabric for wearing comfort.

Albright learned about military life on a visit to the Fort Polk military base in Louisiana. This is the site of the Joint Readiness Training Center, where military people prepare for special services such as UN missions. While she was there, Albright wore camouflage face paint, ate Army MREs (meals ready to eat), and appeared to enjoy being part of the team.

Colin Powell retired as chairman of the Joint Chiefs of Staff that fall. Although he was no longer there to oppose Albright, she was still not able to get the

Albright wore camouflage paint and ate Army MREs (meals ready to eat) when she visited the Joint Readiness Training Center at Fort Polk in Louisiana.

United States to support air strikes in Bosnia. Other foreign policy leaders were not ready to send U.S. soldiers into Bosnia. Albright had an explanation for this difference of opinion. "My mind-set is Munich," she has said. "Most of my generation's was Vietnam."[7]

"Munich" refers to the Munich Pact signed by European leaders in 1938. That agreement opened the door for Hitler to invade Czechoslovakia. Albright was just a toddler when that agreement was signed. She was too young to understand what it meant. But her father did remember, and she had heard him talk about it. For Albright, the Munich Pact was a sign of weakness. European countries had an opportunity to act against Hitler, but they chose not to get involved. The result was World War II.

Other leaders in U.S. foreign policy were coming from a different background. In the 1960s and 1970s, the United States fought an unpopular war in Vietnam. Because of that war, Americans had formed an attitude of not wanting to get involved in foreign conflicts. They were reminded of that when American soldiers were killed in Somalia. They did not want that to happen in Bosnia. President Clinton said that he would not authorize air strikes in the former Yugoslavia without the approval of Congress. That would not happen soon.

It was a disappointment for Albright, but it did not dampen her enthusiasm for her work as ambassador. When she was asked how she liked her job, she said, "It's like being in a candy store."[8]

The year ahead would be even sweeter. It marked some important highlights in her career.

7

A Tough-Talking Cowgirl

In January 1994, Albright flew to the Czech Republic with President Clinton on *Air Force One*. She later talked about how she felt standing next to Clinton as they were greeted by Czech president Vaclav Havel. There she was with the leader of the country where she was born and the leader of the country that gave her family safety from communism. "It doesn't get any better than this," she said.[1]

That same month, Albright made a trip to Croatia, part of the former Yugoslavia. She visited what had at one time been a garbage dump. Now it was a mass-grave site. It was estimated that two hundred bodies were buried there. They were Croats who had been killed by the Yugoslav Army.

Serbs made up much of the Yugoslav Army. At the United Nations, Albright had pushed for a resolution to hold hearings and punish the Serbian military leaders who committed these war crimes. That resolution was passed. So far, however, United Nations forces had not been successful in capturing any of those leaders. Albright continued to speak out against these crimes, keeping people aware of what was happening. Her actions made Serbs angry.

Albright was walking outside the United Nations in New York one day when a gray-haired woman shouted at her. "Why are you so awful to the Serbs?"[2]

Albright is accompanied by U.S. soldiers in the former Yugoslavia. She was very outspoken about the war crimes being committed in that country by Serbian military leaders.

The woman was speaking Serbo-Croatian, but Albright knew some of the language. She answered the woman in Serbo-Croatian. "Because they *are* awful," she said.[3]

Early in her career, Albright earned a reputation as someone who gets the job done. As ambassador, she proved that she still had that ability. One of her greatest moments came in 1994 when she pushed for a military invasion in Haiti.

Haiti and the Dominican Republic share the island of Hispaniola, which is near Cuba. In Haiti, a military leader had taken control of the government away from the democratically elected president, Jean-Bertrand Aristide. The new government began to get rid of people who did not support it. Haitian citizens were rounded up and thrown into prison. Others tried to escape by crowding into small boats headed for Florida. Tragically, many of them drowned when their overloaded boats capsized.

Albright said that the United States should use military force to unseat the military ruler in Haiti. Other foreign policy leaders did not think that would be possible. The United States would not send its military into another country without approval from the United Nations. People in the State Department did not think that the United Nations would approve such an action.[4]

Albright disagreed. "If I have the authority, I think I can do it," she told President Clinton.[5] Clinton told her to try.

Albright met with each of the representatives in the Security Council and persuaded them to vote in favor of military action. On July 31, 1994, the Security Council approved Resolution 940. It allowed the United States to lead an invasion of Haiti to unseat the military dictatorship. Then Albright gave the military ruler from Haiti a choice: "You can depart voluntarily and soon or involuntarily and soon."[6]

Her statement reminded some people of the tough-talking cowboy heroes from old western movies. One magazine published a cartoon showing Albright wearing a cowboy hat and six-guns. Albright framed the cartoon and hung it on her office wall.

Part of the cartoon was true. Albright owns several of the Stetson hats that cowboys made popular, and she likes to wear them.

Although Albright was known to get the job done, some members of the Security Council did not like the way she did it. They said she broke one of the rules of diplomacy. Ambassadors talk to one another about foreign policy, then they each report back to their own president or prime minister. It is not considered proper for an ambassador of one country to go directly to the leader of another country.

Albright did not worry about what was proper. She did what she needed to do to get results. An example was when she pushed to keep economic sanctions against Iraq in effect. These sanctions had been in place since the Gulf War. They were not to be lifted until Iraqi president Saddam Hussein followed through on the peace agreement reached at the end of that war. Part of the agreement was that Saddam would not rebuild his arsenal of weapons.

By 1994, France, China, and Russia wanted to relax the sanctions, especially those forbidding delivery of medical supplies. They said that Iraqi civilians, mostly children, were dying from malnutrition and preventable diseases as a result of the sanctions. Albright said that the sanctions needed to be kept in place because Saddam was hiding weapons. She flew to the capitals of most of the remaining eleven countries on the Security Council, showing the leaders of those countries photos of those weapons. The photos had been taken by members of the Central Intelligence Agency (CIA), whose purpose is to provide the president with foreign intelligence—top secret information about U.S. enemies or potential enemies.

Members of the Security Council did not like Albright's going over their heads this way, but Albright accomplished what she set out to do. The sanctions were kept in place.

Albright's critics noted that she sometimes did not sound very diplomatic, either. One time, she disagreed with a speech given at the United Nations by the Iraqi deputy prime minister. She called it "one of the most ridiculous" speeches she had ever heard.[7] Another time, she told the defense minister from France to mind his own business.

Some ambassadors complained because Albright did not attend all the social activities at the United Nations. Sometimes when she did attend, it was only to put in a short appearance. The United Nations often has receptions in honor of important world leaders. These events are noted for their elegant buffet tables of food. Albright says she does not have time for these activities. "I have been sent here by my Government to eat," she joked at one reception.[8] Then she left without eating and went back to her office to work.

Albright does not seem to mind the criticism. In fact, sometimes she appears to enjoy it. An Iraqi newspaper called Albright a serpent because of her determination to keep sanctions in place. Later, Albright showed up at the Security Council wearing a brooch in the shape of a serpent. Another Iraqi supporter called her a witch and sent her a broom. Albright displayed the broom in her office.

In a televised interview, news correspondent Barbara Walters asked Albright how she felt about the criticism. "Do you care?" Walters wondered.[9]

"No," Albright said. She noted that her only concern was that she said what needed to be said.[10]

By October 1994, Aristide, the democratic president of Haiti, was back in power. American soldiers were still stationed on the island for peacekeeping. Albright spent Thanksgiving there, joining the soldiers for dinner.

In 1995, the United Nations celebrated its fiftieth anniversary. Albright planned a tour to observe that occasion. She went to six U.S. cities to talk about the importance of the United Nations. Albright has said that it is hard to make Americans understand that what happens in other countries affects people in the United States.

She says foreign policy includes many issues, such as drugs, terrorism, international crime, the environment, and human rights. Something that

Albright holds a Haitian infant at the Port-au-Prince Airport in Haiti in 1994. With Albright is Defense Secretary William J. Perry. Albright celebrated Thanksgiving with the American soldiers stationed in Haiti for peacekeeping.

happens in the Middle East, which has large supplies of oil, can affect the price of gasoline in the United States. Foreign trade creates more jobs for American people. A good relationship with other countries means that Americans can do business and travel safely in those countries.

Albright was soon talking about women's rights and foreign policy. In September 1995, she attended a United Nations conference on women's issues. Before the conference, a writer for *Glamour* magazine interviewed Albright. The reporter asked Albright how issues such as birth control can affect foreign policy. Albright explained that a country that cannot feed its growing population has conflicts. Those conflicts can spill over borders into other countries.

In the *Glamour* magazine interview, Albright also talked about how hard it is for a woman to be treated as an equal with men in a field like foreign relations, where there are few women. "Even at my level—and I feel that I've finally made it—you have to prove every day that you know what you're talking about," she said.[11]

However, she often jokes about the advantages of being a woman. One big advantage, she says, is makeup. "When you're absolutely exhausted, you can go paint on a different face and be okay," she said.[12]

Once, at a diplomatic dinner, she discovered another advantage to being a woman. When it came time for photographs, Albright saw that she had spilled something on the front of her skirt. She simply turned her skirt around, so that the spot was in back for the photo. Then she joked that men did not have it so easy.

She did make one small change when she became ambassador. She stopped carrying a purse. "I kept leaving it under tables," she explained.[13] Actually, she no longer *had* to carry a purse. She now had aides to haul things for her. She said that some of her male aides were uncomfortable about carrying her lipstick at first, but they adjusted.

In the fall of 1995, Colin Powell's autobiography, *My American Journey*, was published. In that book he wrote about his disagreement with Albright over air strikes in Bosnia, but the situation had changed since then. During 1994 and 1995, the violence had continued in Bosnia and the United States got involved. The air strikes that Albright had called for in 1993 were finally carried out. In fact, some of the most serious strikes were made the week Powell's book was released. "Maybe he'd want to rewrite that page now," Albright said, referring to what Powell wrote about her in his book.[14]

The air strikes convinced Bosnian Serbs that it was time to find a peaceful settlement. Albright was given credit for bringing them to the bargaining table. It was a huge victory for her. "I think Bosnia was a turning point," one of Albright's friends told a reporter. "Until then, she still thought of herself—at least, a little bit—as a divorced housewife. But on the most important foreign-policy question of the first term she was right and the guys were wrong."[15]

By now, Americans were used to their blunt-talking UN ambassador. But Albright soon managed to surprise them with even tougher words.

8

"Madeleine Albright's Audition"

In February 1996, Cuban air force pilots shot down two unarmed civilian planes. The planes carried members of a Miami-based group of Cuban exiles called Brothers to the Rescue, which protested against the Cuban government. Now it appeared that military planes had shot down innocent civilians just to silence them. Albright called it "cold-blooded murder."[1]

She was especially angry after hearing a recording of the conversation that the Cuban pilots had in the cockpit of their fighter plane. The pilots bragged about their courage in shooting down the planes. The word they used was *cojones* (Spanish for testicles).

At the United Nations, Albright responded.

"Frankly, this is not *cojones*," she said. "This is cowardice."[2]

That comment brought mixed reactions. Some people were shocked by her vulgarity. "She tried to say a man's word, and it was uncalled for," one former diplomat said.[3] On the other hand, many Cuban-Americans made her their hero. They even had bumper stickers made up with her words on them.

On March 2, Albright represented President Clinton at a memorial service for the Cuban exiles who were killed. The service was held at the Orange Bowl in Miami, Florida. Albright, who usually dressed in brightly colored suits, wore black, the color of mourning, for her appearance at the Orange Bowl.

More than sixty thousand Cuban-Americans attended the service. They stood and cheered for Albright. "Madeleine, *libertad*!" they called.[4] *Libertad* is the Spanish word for liberty or freedom. They applauded loudly and often, making it hard for Albright to finish her speech.

Albright got a much different reception when she toured the Croatian city of Vukovar later that month. Croatia is part of the former Yugoslavia. In 1991, Serbs had captured Vukovar. As part of the peace settlement in the former Yugoslavia, the city was about to be returned to Croatia. Mobs of angry Serbs shouted obscenities at Albright as she and her aides walked through the streets.

Albright would not let the crowd know that she was bothered by this disturbance. She held her head high and told her aides "to walk with dignity."[5] Later, people threw stones at Albright's motorcade, breaking two windows in one of the cars. No one was injured, but it was a tense time for everyone in the motorcade.

In July, Albright traveled to the city of Prague in the Czech Republic with First Lady Hillary Rodham Clinton. For four days Albright was Mrs. Clinton's tour guide. They shopped, visited historic sights, and spent time with Czech president Vaclav Havel. Albright also shared some of her personal history with Mrs. Clinton, showing Clinton the yellow house where she lived as a child.

Albright said she was just being a friend. Others said the trip was much more. President Clinton was running for reelection in 1996, and Secretary of State Warren Christopher was expected to retire. Many people thought that Albright would replace him. Reporters noted that Hillary Clinton would like a woman to become secretary of state. When the two women traveled to Prague together, it seemed that Albright was being considered for that position. In fact, one reporter, who covered the trip for *The New York Times*, titled her article "Madeleine Albright's Audition."[6]

President Clinton was reelected in 1996 and Secretary of State Warren Christopher announced his retirement. Rumors began to fly as people wondered who would get his job.

At that time, Albright was in the middle of a power struggle at the United Nations. Boutros Boutros-Ghali was coming to the end of his first term as secretary-general, the head of the United Nations. The secretary-general is elected to a five-year term, but is

Albright served as tour guide for First Lady Hillary Clinton when the two women visited Prague, in the Czech Republic.

eligible to run for a second term. Boutros-Ghali had decided to do so.

Members of the United States Congress were not happy with his decision. They wanted Boutros-Ghali to step down. They had turned against him after the deaths of the eighteen U.S. soldiers in Somalia in October 1992. They blamed Boutros-Ghali for that episode. They said he was the one who had turned that peacekeeping operation into a mission to capture Somali warlords. They also said that he had not cut the operating budget of the United Nations as he had promised he would do during his first term. Boutros-Ghali had made cuts in the budget, but his critics said he had not made enough.

Albright said that she admired Boutros-Ghali as a person. But she, too, had disagreed with him on some issues, especially Bosnia. He wanted United Nations control; she wanted NATO control.

According to reports, Clinton gave Albright the assignment of making sure that Boutros-Ghali was not reelected. Albright's aides thought it was an impossible task. "Anything we're asked to do, we will do," she told her aides.[7] Then she went to work.

Albright met one-on-one with UN representatives from countries that were friendly with the United States. At these meetings she convinced them that it would be a good idea to let her have her way this time. It would determine how well their countries and the United States would work together in the future.

On December 4, 1996, Boutros-Ghali announced that he would not seek reelection. It was a victory for Albright, but it did not make her popular with many

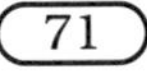

people at the United Nations. They called her a bully for her part in seeing that Boutros-Ghali was not reelected.

The next day, Clinton nominated Madeleine Albright for the position of secretary of state. Clinton and Albright appeared together at a press conference to make that announcement. Clinton spoke first. He talked about Albright's childhood and how it had shaped her views on foreign policy. "She watched her world fall apart, and ever since, she has dedicated her life to spreading to the rest of the world the freedom and tolerance her family found here in America," he said.[8]

Then Albright accepted the nomination. Albright, who was wearing her usual high-heeled shoes, turned to Warren Christopher and said, "I can only hope my heels can fill your shoes."[9]

It was a historic occasion. If the Senate approved Albright's nomination, she would be the first woman to become secretary of state. In spite of the importance of the occasion, one reporter chose to write about what Albright wore that day. The reporter said that Albright was too heavy to wear a bright red suit.

Albright likes the press and is usually willing to answer their questions. But there are some things, she says, that should be off-limits to reporters. She does not want to pick up the morning paper and see an article about how she looks or what she wore. She says that when she is working, she does not have time to worry about how she looks.

Albright also does not like it when reporters ask her about being a single woman. They wonder if she

President Bill Clinton and Vice President Al Gore, Jr., look on as Albright accepts her nomination as secretary of state.

is lonely being on her own. Albright says that is something they would never ask a man in her position.

Although Albright does not like that question, she has answered it. In a television interview, Barbara Walters asked, "Is there any room for a man in your life or romance in your life?"[10]

"Sure, but I think that it's probably not the easiest thing for somebody to kind of fit in with my crazy schedule," Albright answered. Then she smiled and added, "But occasionally somebody does."[11]

After accepting the nomination, the next step for Albright was to prepare for her confirmation hearing before the Senate in January. Albright needed the approval of two thirds of the Senate to be appointed secretary of state. Most people appeared to like Clinton's choice for the position, but Albright did have some critics.

One of the reasons Clinton nominated Albright for secretary of state was that she could explain his foreign policy in a way that others could understand. Ironically, this was exactly what her critics used against her. They said she was a good salesperson for foreign policy, but she did not have much experience in *forming* foreign policy. It was a criticism that had followed her throughout her career.

Critics also noted that although Albright was an expert on Europe, she did not have a lot of experience with Asia. However, she had traveled in many other countries as UN ambassador. Many people believed that her travel had prepared her for working with other parts of the world.

Albright appeared before the Senate for her confirmation hearing in January 1997. The hearing was interrupted by five activists who protested the economic sanctions against Iraq that had been in effect since the Gulf War. They said that because of the sanctions, the children in Iraq were starving.

Security guards quickly got the demonstrators out of the room, but Albright went ahead and answered their accusations. "I am as concerned about the children of Iraq as anyone in this room," she said.[12] She went on to say that the person who was responsible for those children was Iraqi dictator Saddam Hussein.

In spite of the interruption, the hearing went well. Albright talked about foreign policy issues such as illegal drug trafficking, terrorism, and human rights. She also made it clear that she was not planning to change her diplomatic style. "I'm going to tell it like it is here, and I'm going to tell it like it is when I go abroad," she said.[13]

That seemed to be all right with the senators. Ninety-nine out of one hundred of its members later voted yes for Albright as secretary of state. The other senator was away on business and could not vote. He later said that if he had been in town, he would have voted yes.

People said that Albright's approval came easily. Albright did not agree. She said that it looked easy because she had prepared for it. "My Christmas vacation was a little like college, when everybody went skiing, and I sat and studied," she explained.[14]

Albright's three daughters were on hand for her

Madeleine Albright with her three daughters—from left, Alice, Anne, and Katie.

swearing-in ceremony on January 23, 1997. The twins, Anne and Alice, were now thirty-five years old. Anne, a lawyer, lived near Washington, D.C. Alice had chosen a career in finance and was living and working in London, England. Twenty-nine-year-old Katie was also a lawyer, living in San Francisco. Albright also had two grandchildren.

Albright joked with her daughters, reminding them that as a mother she had worried about where they were and what they were doing. That had changed. Part of Albright's job would be to travel throughout the world, meeting with the leaders of other countries. "Now you will have the chance to worry about me," Albright told her daughters.[15]

As secretary of state, Albright would serve on the National Security Council and foreign policy committees. She would also head the State Department, which employs more than twenty-five thousand people. This includes the ambassadors in United States embassies all over the world and the U.S. ambassador to the United Nations. Albright would advise the president on choosing ambassadors and other diplomatic representatives. She would also be in charge of the Great Seal of the United States. The State Department publishes federal laws and puts the Great Seal on them to show that they are official. The State Department also issues passports to Americans who travel to other countries.

There was a lot of work to do, and Albright was ready to start. When a reporter asked Albright how she felt about her new job, she said, "I am very glad to be here. There's a whole bunch of things to tackle and I am all set to go."[16]

9

The Mystery of Albright's Past

Albright quickly got down to the business of being secretary of state. After her swearing-in ceremony, she and President Clinton had a meeting with Kofi Annan, the new secretary-general of the United Nations. She followed that with a briefing on United States relations with China.

The following day, Albright appeared on *Larry King Live*, a CNN cable television interview show. She also held a press conference announcing that in February she would make a whirlwind tour through Europe and Asia. Final plans for the trip still needed to be made.

That evening, Albright hosted a reception. Among the invited guests were friends, family, members of the press, politicians, and diplomats. The guest list was so long that the reception had to be divided into two shifts.

Many people noted that Albright's views on foreign policy were similar to those of former secretary Warren Christopher. But there were huge differences in their styles. An obvious difference was that Albright was a woman. That was something she playfully pointed out during her first meeting with the State Department staff. She stepped out from behind the podium, curtsied, and said, "You may notice that I don't exactly look like Secretary Christopher."[1]

Albright told her staff that she would say exactly what was on her mind. "I don't shilly-shally much," she said. "I don't say 'on the one hand, on the other hand.'"[2]

She also warned her staff that she was not concerned about people's positions. "I make phone calls to people that are not directly below me," she explained.[3] That was not a surprise to her staff. Even if they did not know her personally, they knew her by reputation. Albright did not worry about going over someone's head or stepping on someone's toes.

On the other hand, Albright encouraged her staff to bring her their good ideas. She made herself more available to staff members by occasionally eating in the State Department cafeteria. But Albright left no doubt about who was in charge. One of her first jobs was to appoint her own people to key positions within the department. As she was putting her team together, she told an aide to remind one appointee that she was the one he would report to.

People were fascinated with their new blunt-talking, tell-it-like-it-is secretary of state. In fact, there was so much interest in her that the State Department had to set up a rotating schedule for reporters. It is similar to what is used for the president of the United States. Reporters dug to find out everything they could about Madeleine Albright. What was she like as a child? Were there signs even then that she would one day rise to a position such as secretary of state?

In the process of finding out more about Albright, Michael Dobbs, a reporter for *The Washington Post* made a surprising discovery. He learned that although Albright had been raised as a Catholic, her parents and grandparents had been Jews. Three of her grandparents had died in concentration camps during the Holocaust. (Albright's maternal grandfather had died before the war.) The information came from Nazi documents that were now held by researchers of the Holocaust. Dobbs had also interviewed Albright's cousin, Dagmar Simova, and old family friends in the former Czechoslovakia. Simova had lived with Albright's family in London during World War II.

Albright discussed Dobbs's findings with Barry Schweid, an Associated Press State Department correspondent. "This .obviously was a major surprise to me," she said. "I had never been told this."[4]

Albright said that this new information about her family's background was a private matter. It affected not only her but also others in her family, including her three daughters and her two young grandsons. Albright said she hoped people would respect their privacy and allow her time to do her own investigation. "I thought that the right way to do this would be to check it out and then have a family discussion," she explained.[5]

However, it seemed that the story was too big to be ignored. There were too many questions. How could Albright not have known about her past? Why had her parents never told her the truth?

Dagmar Simova had one explanation. When the family returned to Prague after the war, Albright was only eight years old. Simova said that perhaps Albright's parents thought that she was too young to understand. For that same reason, Albright said she never really wondered how her grandparents had died. "If you're eight years old and you are told that your grandparents died and you think of grandparents as being old people then you don't question it," she said.[6]

That still did not explain why her parents did not tell her about her ancestors or their own backgrounds when she was older. Only Albright's parents knew their *real* reasons, but neither of them was still living. Her father had died in 1977 and her mother in 1989.

Some people suggested that Albright had known the truth all along, but was trying to hide it. Others knew that the situation was more common than most people realized. According to reports, there were thousands of people who found out years after the war that their parents had been Jewish. Their parents had also made the decision not to tell their children the truth.

"If your family went through what went on in

Albright speaks to Leo Pavlat, the director of the Prague Jewish Museum. Shortly after becoming secretary of state, Albright learned that her grandparents were Jewish and that three of them had died in concentration camps during the Holocaust.

Europe in the late 1930s and 1940s, you could understand," one writer explained. "It was a question of survival."[7] At that time, Hitler was killing Jews in Europe. Once the decision had been made, to hide the fact that they were Jews, it seemed best to leave their past behind them. Or perhaps it was just too painful to think about.

Even with these explanations, people wondered why Albright had never figured out the details of her past on her own. She did admit that she had received letters from people in Czechoslovakia when she became ambassador to the United Nations. At that time, because of her position, her name began appearing in newspapers. Albright did not pay too much attention to the letters because she said the facts did not go together. For example, one letter said that she had been born in Belgrade in the former Yugoslavia.

On the other hand, the letters did make Albright suspect that her parents may have been Jews. Newspeople reported that she was surprised when she found out about her Jewish background. Albright said those reports were not accurate. "I was not surprised about my Jewish origin. What I was surprised about was that my grandparents died in concentration camps," she said.[8]

Albright did not have time to look into this new information about her background. She was too busy with her new duties as secretary of state. However, her brother and sister went to Prague to see what they could learn.

In the meantime, Albright left for an official tour

through Europe and Asia. The tour was a chance for Albright to meet some foreign leaders and to renew her friendship with others. It also gave her an opportunity to address some pressing foreign relations problems.

One of the countries she visited was China. The United States and China had not been getting along. The United States was interested in improving relations. On the other hand, there was concern about human rights violations that were taking place in China. Albright would have to be tough in letting China know that the United States was against these practices.

People wondered if Chinese leaders would be willing to listen to her. After all, she was a woman. Chinese women did not have leadership roles. Albright said the fact that she was a woman would not matter. She was representing the United States and that was more important. It appeared that she was right. After meeting with Albright, Chinese president Jiang Zemin said that he thought she was someone he could work with.

Another challenge that Albright faced as secretary of state was the issue of expansion of the North Atlantic Treaty Organization (NATO). The countries of Poland, Hungary, and the Czech Republic had applied for membership to NATO. These countries had formerly been part of what was known as the Soviet bloc—a group of Communist countries—which had opposed NATO. They had been allied with the Soviet Union, now Russia and other republics. Albright's challenge would be to find a way to allow these countries membership without creating conflict with Russia.

One of Albright's stops during her tour was Brussels, Belgium, where NATO had its headquarters. There she noted that admitting the three countries to NATO was important for stability in Europe. It could prevent border disputes and ethnic conflicts. She also made a stop in Russia, where she assured Russian leaders that NATO expansion was not intended to be anti-Russian. The Russians were not convinced, but as Albright knew, they could do nothing to stop the process. Foreign ministers of fifteen countries had already shown their support for NATO expansion.

People were used to the fact that Albright's brooches were a sign of how she felt. That was why some reporters thought that it had a special meaning when she got off the plane one day during her tour wearing a black Stetson hat. They said that she was trying to show power by creating the image of "a sheriff riding into town."[9]

It was one of Albright's daughters who figured out the real reason for the hat. Albright was having a bad hair day.

Albright's trip was considered a big success. People liked her energy and her enthusiasm for her new job. She charmed Russian leader Boris Yeltsin by speaking to him in Russian. In France, she answered reporters' questions in English, French, and Russian. In a private meeting with French president Jacques Chirac, she began and ended the meeting in French.

"It's very good that you speak French," Chirac said. "That makes our work much easier."[10]

Traveling to other countries to talk about foreign policy issues was a large part of Albright's new job. But she never went anywhere without preparing fully.

Albright enjoys wearing hats such as this black Stetson. She has also found that the hats come in handy when she is having a bad hair day.

"One of the things that makes me uncomfortable is when I don't have all the facts," she said.[11]

Because she was well prepared, she was able to stand her ground when dealing with foreign leaders who tried to bully her. In June, she traveled to the former Yugoslavia to meet with the Serbian president, Slobodan Milosevic. The Serbian government had violated several parts of the peace agreement reached in 1995. As Albright was listing these violations, Milosevic interrupted. "Madame Secretary, you're not well informed."[12]

Albright did not like his comment. She had lived in Yugoslavia for three years as a child, and she thought she knew the country well. "Don't tell me I'm uninformed," she said. "I lived here."[13]

Albright could be tough, but people sometimes saw another side. In July, she made her first visit to Prague as secretary of state. She visited the Pinkas Synagogue, where the names of her grandparents were listed on a wall. The wall was a memorial to Jews who had died in the Holocaust.

Albright said she now fully understood the difficult decision her parents had made. How hard it must have been for them to leave other family members behind. But that decision had saved her life and gave her freedom. "I will always love and honor my parents and will always respect their decision, for that most painful of choices gave me life a second time," she said.[14]

In addition to her travels to other countries, Albright made trips to cities across the United States, giving talks. It was part of her continuing desire to get

Americans more involved in foreign policy. "One of my prime jobs here is to reconnect the American people to foreign policy and make it understandable," she said.[15]

There were also meetings on Capitol Hill. Albright wanted to convince Congress to increase the foreign policy budget and to pay outstanding dues to the United Nations. She was also determined to have a good working relationship with the Republican-controlled Congress. "It's the right thing to do, but it's also the smart thing to do," she said.[16]

In addition, Albright had regular meetings with other members of Clinton's foreign policy team. She and National Security Advisor Sandy Berger were good friends. They spoke almost daily by phone. On most Mondays, Albright had lunch with Berger and William Cohen, the defense secretary. These meetings were called the ABC meetings, referring to the first letter of each of their last names.

Albright was so busy that people began to wonder if she ever had time to relax. A reporter asked her what she did for fun. Albright said she relaxed on her farm in Virginia. "Nobody would ever recognize me on the farm as I play around in my garden barefooted, and I go to the movies, and I knit," she noted.[17] Her other hobbies include needlepoint and sewing.

She also enjoys shopping. One of her favorite activities is to shop for antiques with one of her friends, the singer-actress Barbra Streisand. The two women met in 1993 when Albright gave a speech at a fund-raising function in Los Angeles. Streisand came to hear what Albright had to say, and the two of them hit it off right away. "We talk about everything: love, relationships, a lot of politics," Streisand said.[18]

However, most of the time Albright worked, and that hard work appeared to be paying off. For the first time in four years, Congress voted in 1997 for an increase in the foreign policy budget. Albright succeeded in pressing the Senate to approve a treaty to ban chemical weapons, and she was able to get Russia to sign a security agreement with NATO. She also got an extension on the deadline for pulling United States troops out of the former Yugoslavia.

United States soldiers were still stationed in Bosnia for peacekeeping. According to the peace agreement made in 1995, the troops were scheduled to leave by June 1998. Albright said that the United States could not meet that deadline and have a lasting peace. There was still too much to do. U.S. soldiers were needed to protect refugees who were returning to their homes. Albright was also determined that those responsible for war crimes against the people of the former Yugoslavia needed to be brought to justice. Seventy-five war criminals had been indicted, but by June 1997, only eight were actually in custody.

President Clinton agreed with Albright. He said that U.S. troops would stay in Bosnia until a lasting peace was established. No deadline was given.

Halfway through Albright's first year as secretary of state, most people said that she was doing a good job. The one criticism was that she had not yet made a trip to the Middle East. That was about to change.

10

A Star in the State Department

The stage was dark except for a single spotlight. It shined on a woman in a black sequined gown. Her back was to the audience. When the music started, she spun around and began to sing. It was Madeleine Albright doing her best imitation of singer/actress Madonna. Albright had a bright yellow scarf wrapped around her neck and a red flower tucked behind her ear to complete the outfit.

The audience was mainly representatives of the Association of Southeast Asian Nations (ASEAN). In August 1997, Albright attended their annual weeklong conference held that year in Malaysia. She had spent several days in long, boring meetings. The final night of the conference featured entertainment performed by the diplomats themselves.

Albright's song was to the tune of Madonna's hit "Don't Cry for Me, Argentina," from the play and movie *Evita*. But the words Albright belted out were "Don't Cry for Me, ASEANies." She had rewritten the lyrics with help from her staff. The new words poked fun at everyone at the conference. Albright's debut as a rock singer got her a three-minute standing ovation. "She was quite a star," one foreign minister said.[1] However, audience members agreed that she was a better diplomat than a singer.

Albright was on her way home from the conference when she received word that thirteen Israelis had been killed in a suicide bombing in Jerusalem. There had been a long history of violence in that part of the the Middle East between Jews and Palestinian Arabs. Starting in the late 1880s, Jews started coming to this area, known then as Palestine, with the idea of building a Jewish state. Between 1933 and 1935, they were joined by more than one hundred thousand Jews from Poland and Germany who were escaping from the Nazis. Palestinian Arabs were not happy—they wanted to make Palestine an Arab state.

In 1947, the UN was called in to help with problems between the Arabs and Jews living in Palestine. The UN divided Palestine into two states, an Arab state and a Jewish state. The Jews accepted the agreement establishing the state of Israel in 1948, but the Palestinian Arabs did not. The neighboring Arab states attacked Israel. Israel won that war and, in the process, took control of some of the land that the UN had originally assigned to the Palestinians.

Israel gained more Palestinian areas in a 1967 war. Meanwhile, the Palestinians and neighboring Arab countries refused to recognize Israel and repeatedly threatened war against it. Some Palestinians engaged in terrorism against Israeli civilians; Israel bombed and shelled Arab villages and refugee camps.

The Israelis and Palestinians were making real progress toward peace in 1995 when an Israeli man opposed to the peace process killed Yitzhak Rabin, Israel's prime minister. Rabin was a strong proponent of peace with the Palestinians. The former secretary of state Warren Christopher had spent a lot of time in the Middle East hoping to bring those countries back to the bargaining table. Albright had yet to make a trip to the area.

Now, with this new outbreak of violence, reporters wanted to know what Albright would do. They asked her if this new development would force her to get involved in the Middle East. Albright did not like the question. "Let me make this clear: I am directly involved in this," she said. "I have been since I became secretary of state."[2] In fact, Albright had already made plans to travel there in September 1997.

A week before Albright's trip to the Middle East, more violence broke out. Three bombs were set off in a Jerusalem shopping area, killing seven people and injuring almost two hundred others. The following day, Israeli soldiers attacked the neighboring Arab country of Lebanon. Some people thought that

Albright should delay her trip until things calmed down a bit. She would not change her plans. "We cannot give in to terror," she said.[3]

Albright met with Palestinian and Israeli leaders to persuade them to renew peace talks. She appeared on Israeli television and spoke to the Palestinian people in a radio address. But in spite of her best efforts, Albright went home disappointed. She said the leaders were not ready to discuss peace. She vowed that she would not come back until they were. "I am not going to come back here just to tread water," she said.[4]

Albright had another letdown a couple of months later. She had worked hard to persuade Congress to approve legislation to pay the outstanding dues owed to the United Nations by the United States. In November, it appeared that the measure would finally be passed. Then, at the last minute, the House rejected it.

Albright's aides said that was her biggest disappointment in her first year as secretary of state. She knew that the United States had lost the respect of other countries because it was not paying its UN dues. The situation affected the ability of United States diplomats to do their work.

That month, Albright also began another battle with an old enemy—President Saddam Hussein of Iraq. According to intelligence reports, Iraq had a large stock of chemical weapons. This was a violation of the peace agreement reached after the Gulf War.

The United Nations had sent a team of about seventy inspectors to Iraq to search for weapons. Six were Americans. In a sudden move, Saddam ordered all the American inspectors out of his country. Members of the United Nations said that Saddam could not dictate which inspectors he would allow into the country. They voted to pull all of the inspectors out until they could reach some kind of an agreement with Saddam.

Saddam's failure to cooperate made it appear likely that he had weapons he did not want the inspectors to find. Now he was keeping the inspectors from doing their job. Something had to be done.

President Clinton said that the first priority for the United States was to find a diplomatic solution to the problem. On the other hand, he said that the United States would use force if it were needed. Clinton ordered aircraft carriers into the Gulf area to be ready for that possibility.

Albright left on November 16, 1997, for a trip to the Gulf countries of Saudi Arabia, Bahrain, and Kuwait. Those countries had been United States allies during the Gulf War, but they were against using force against Iraq this time. Some people thought that Albright's trip was an attempt to change the minds of leaders from those countries. Albright said that was not the case. "I am going to Saudi Arabia because they are very close friends and because we have a mutual interest in the stability of the region," she said.[5]

In the meantime, United Nations representatives worked to find a diplomatic solution. On November 20, 1997, after an emergency middle-of-the-night meeting of the Security Council, it appeared that they

At this session of the UN Security Council on Africa, Albright sits next to Koffi Annan, the secretary-general of the United Nations. Albright worked closely with Annan to bring an end to a crisis between the United States and Iraq.

had reached an agreement with Iraq. Secretary of State Madeleine Albright made a statement to the press. She said that Iraq was expected to announce that United States inspectors would be allowed back into the country. However, Albright was not sure that would happen. "I will believe it when I see it," she said.[6]

Albright was right to have doubts. In the next few months, it appeared that Saddam was interested only in delays. In January 1998, he said that he would not cooperate with UN inspectors unless economic sanctions were lifted. He also accused one of the U.S. inspectors of being a spy. The United States continued building its military forces in the Gulf region. It appeared more than ever that the United States was headed toward a conflict with Iraq. Many Americans were against such action.

Albright began traveling in the United States to talk to Americans about the situation. On February 18, she appeared at Ohio State University in Columbus, Ohio. Defense Secretary William Cohen and National Security Advisor Sandy Berger made the trip with Albright, but she was the first to speak to the crowd of about six thousand people.

She was interrupted several times during her speech by protesters who chanted, "One-two-three-four, we don't want your racist war."[7] It was a reminder of the antiwar protests on campuses all across the United States during the Vietnam War. The meeting was televised live by CNN, allowing millions of Americans to watch from their homes.

The following day on *Good Morning America*, Albright was asked if she thought that the meeting was a mistake. "No, I think it was a good idea," she answered. "I think it's very important for us to be able to talk to the American people. We will continue to do that."[8] Albright noted that the protesters were in the minority at that meeting. She said that others asked well-thought-out questions. A criticism of Albright was that she did not do a good job of answering those questions and appeared defensive.

Albright got a different reception on the University of South Carolina campus on February 19. There were a few protesters outside the building where she spoke that day. However, the students, who gathered inside to hear her lecture, gave her a standing ovation.

What protesters did not know was that, behind the scenes, Albright was also working on a diplomatic answer. Kofi Annan, the secretary-general of the United Nations, flew to Iraq to meet with Saddam on February 22, 1998. Before that trip, Albright had been very busy drawing up a list of points that the United States would insist upon in an agreement with Iraq. After meetings with Annan, Saddam eventually agreed to all of those points.

Most people did not believe that would be a lasting agreement, and they were right. In the summer of 1998, Saddam again refused to allow inspectors into the country. Once again, Albright said that the United States would not back down from a conflict with Iraq.

In July 1998, Albright was inducted into the National Women's Hall of Fame. The Hall of Fame is located in Seneca Falls, New York, where the first Women's Rights Convention was held in 1848. The organization honors women who have made an important contribution in advancing the roles of women. Speaking at that induction ceremony, Albright noted that she was proud that more women were now involved in U.S. foreign policy.

The following month, Albright was once again faced with another serious foreign relations problem. On August 7, 1998, terrorists bombed U.S. embassies in the African countries of Kenya and Tanzania. Twelve Americans were among the 257 people killed.

In an interview on NBC's *Meet the Press*, Albright warned that the United States would strike back if necessary.

For the next two weeks, U.S. intelligence agencies investigated to find out who was responsible for the bombings. In the meantime, the bodies of ten of the Americans killed were flown to Germany. Albright went to Germany and brought back the bodies. The following week, she visited the places where the bombings took place. Americans had seen television coverage of the scenes, but Albright said those pictures could not show the real horror. "They're nowhere near what it's really like when you're in the buildings and you see bloody hand prints," she explained.[9]

On August 20, the United States retaliated. U.S. forces fired more than seventy-five cruise missiles in two separate attacks. One of the targets was a well-known terrorist camp in Afghanistan. At that time, several terrorist groups were gathering at the camp for a meeting. The other target was a pharmaceutical plant in the African country of Sudan. According to intelligence reports, chemical weapons were being manufactured there.

After the attack, Albright explained why the United States had to respond to this terrorist attack. "The world—and the terrorists—are watching now to see whether America retreats or continues to lead. Let them have no illusions. We will not be intimidated," she said.[10] However, later investigations cast doubts that chemical weapons had actually been manufactured at the Sudanese plant.

Finding solutions to world problems is not easy, nor quick. In 1998, Albright noted that the problem between India and Pakistan that her father had worked on fifty years earlier had still not been resolved. Albright's efforts in support of peace in the Middle East continued to frustrate her, with no real progress. At the end of 1998, the United States once again launched air strikes against Iraq, after Iraqi president Saddam Hussein refused to cooperate with UN weapons inspectors.

Problems also continued in the Balkans, this time in the Yugoslav province of Kosovo. About 90 percent of the 2 million people in Kosovo were ethnic Albanians. They wanted to declare their independence from the Yugoslav state of Serbia. Yugoslavian president Slobodan Milosevic wanted Kosovo to remain a part of Serbia.

Albright played a key role in trying to negotiate a peaceful solution between the Albanians and the Serbs. But when reports began to spread of the slaughter of innocent Albanians, Albright warned Milosevic that NATO would strike if the killing of Albanian civilians did not stop. He ignored those warnings. On March 24, 1999, the United States joined forces with other NATO countries in launching air attacks on Kosovo.

While NATO bombs rained down on Kosovo, the world watched in horror as Albanians were driven from that province by Serb soldiers.

Some people blamed Albright—and the NATO bombing—for the fate of these refugees. Albright heard the criticism, but it did not stop her from doing what she felt was right. "I would rather be out front and criticized for saving lives than sitting back and waiting for somebody else to state the case," she said. "I mean, I come out of a Europe where I felt great wrong had been done because good people waited too long to try to figure out what to do . . . I do believe in American power."[11]

Although people do not always agree with Albright, she has managed to get Americans interested in foreign relations again. Her unusual diplomatic style has earned her fans. Albright likes to tell about one of her favorite fan letters. It was from a young girl who

Albright's unusual diplomatic style has revived American interest in foreign policy.

explained that at her school, her teacher had the students tell whose shoes they would like to be in. The girl picked Albright. Although the teacher was referring to a popular saying that meant whose place the students would like to be in, the girl took it more literally. She wrote to Albright and asked her for a pair of shoes. Albright sent her a pair.

Albright has become a role model for many young women, and she encourages all young people to learn more about what is happening in the world around them. She says they can do that by reading newspapers and news magazines. She also tells them to learn a foreign language. "Most importantly," she says, "set your sights as high as possible and pursue every opportunity."[12] It is the same advice that she has followed on her road to a successful career in foreign relations.

Chronology

1937—Marie Jana Korbel (later, "Madeleine") is born on May 15 in Prague, Czechoslovakia.

1939—Czechoslovakia is invaded by Hitler's Nazi troops; Korbel family escapes to safety in London.

1948—Korbel family is given political asylum in the United States.

1955—Graduates from high school; enrolls at Wellesley College in Wellesley, Massachusetts.

1959—Earns a B.A. degree in political science, graduating with honors from Wellesley College; marries Joseph Albright on June 11.

1961—Twin daughters, Anne and Alice, are born.

1967—Daughter Katherine is born.

1968—Earns a master's degree in political science and a certificate in Russian studies from Columbia University.

1976—Earns a doctoral degree in political science from Columbia University; becomes chief legislative assistant to U.S. Senator Edmund S. Muskie.

1977—Josef Korbel, her father, dies.

1978—Joins the National Security Council staff.

1981—Receives a fellowship at the Woodrow Wilson International Center for Scholars at the Smithsonian Institution; serves as senior fellow in Soviet and Eastern European affairs at the Center for Strategic and International Studies.

1982—Divorced from husband; becomes a professor of international affairs at Georgetown University.

1989—Anna Korbel, her mother, dies.

1989–1992—Serves as president of the Center for National Policy.

1993–1996—Is U.S. ambassador to the United Nations.

1997—Becomes secretary of state.

1998—Inducted into the National Women's Hall of Fame.

Chapter Notes

Chapter 1. Telling It Like It Is

1. Matthew Cooper and Melinda Liu, "Bright Light," *Newsweek*, February 10, 1997, p. 23.
2. Ibid.
3. Alain L. Sanders, "Brooching the Subject Diplomatically," *Time*, March 24, 1997, p. 36.
4. Ibid.
5. Larry King, interview with Madeleine K. Albright, *Larry King Live*, CNN, January 24, 1997.

Chapter 2. "A Born Leader"

1. Michael Dobbs, "Albright's Family Tragedy Comes to Light," *The Washington Post*, February 4, 1997, p. A8.
2. Nancy Gibbs, "The Many Lives of Madeleine," *Time*, February 17, 1997, p. 58.
3. Michael Dobbs, "Out of the Past," *The Washington Post Magazine*, February 9, 1997, p. 18.
4. Ibid.
5. Ibid.
6. Madeleine K. Albright, "Message From the Secretary of State," *The Mini Page*, March 17, 1997, p. 4.
7. Julia Reed, "Woman of the World," *Vogue*, September 1997, p. 644.
8. Gibbs, p. 54.
9. Albright, p. 4.
10. Ed Bradley, interview with Madeleine K. Albright, *Sixty Minutes*, CBS-TV, February 9, 1997.
11. Gibbs, p. 60.

Chapter 3. Dr. Albright

1. Susan Baer, "A Passion for Foreign Policy," *Baltimore Sun*, January 5, 1997, p. A9.
2. Julia Reed, "Woman of the World," *Vogue*, September 1997, p. 641.
3. Ibid.
4. Ibid., p. 726.

5. Molly Sinclair, "Woman on Top of the World," *The Washington Post*, January 6, 1991, p. F4.

6. Ibid.

Chapter 4. "Shoot, Sit, or Negotiate"

1. Anne Albright, "Your Mom's on the Floor With the Senator, Kids," *Newsweek*, February 10, 1997, p. 26.

2. Ibid.

3. Michael Dobbs and John M. Goshko, "Albright's Personal Odyssey Shaped Foreign Policy Beliefs," *The Washington Post*, December 6, 1996, p. A25.

4. Elaine Sciolino, "Madeleine Albright's Audition," *The New York Times Magazine*, September 22, 1996, p. 104.

5. Molly Sinclair, "Woman on Top of the World," *The Washington Post*, January 6, 1991, p. F4.

6. Susan Baer, "A Passion for Foreign Policy," *Baltimore Sun*, January 5, 1997, p. A8.

7. Geraldine Baum, "A Diplomatic Core," *Los Angeles Times*, February 8, 1995, p. F11.

8. Joan Vennochi, "Dukakis' Foreign Aide: Albright's Approach Is Pragmatic," *The Boston Globe*, May 13, 1998, p. 47.

9. Julia Reed, "Woman of the World," *Vogue*, September 1997, p. 642.

10. Jacob Heilbrunn, "Albright's Mission," *The New Republic*, August 22 and 29, 1994, p. 24.

11. Vennochi, p. 47.

12. Ibid.

13. Sciolino, p. 64.

14. Craig R. Whitney, "In the East, the Selling of Democracy Takes On a New Fervor," *The New York Times*, January 21, 1990, p. A14.

15. Sinclair, p. F4.

Chapter 5. "What You See Is What You Get"

1. Jacob Heilbrunn, "Albright's Mission," *The New Republic*, August 22 and 29, 1994, p. 24.

2. Dan Balz, "U.N. Post Will Complete Odyssey for Albright: Daughter of Czech Diplomat Has Both Academic and Campaign Credentials," *The Washington Post*, December 23, 1992, p. A10.

3. Thomas Blood, *Madam Secretary: A Biography of Madeleine Albright* (New York: St. Martin's Press, 1997), p. 84.

4. Geraldine Baum, "A Diplomatic Core," *Los Angeles Times*, February 8, 1995, p. F10.

5. Lee Michael Katz, "U.N. Ambassador Lives a Tale of Two Cities: Job Has New Status, Influence," *USA Today*, April 8, 1993, p. 6A.

6. Kevin Fedarko, "Clinton's Blunt Instrument," *Time*, October 31, 1994, p. 31.

7. Nancy Gibbs, "Voice of America," *Time*, December 16, 1996, p. 33.

8. Barbara Crossette, "Albright Makes Her U.N. Post a Focal Point," *The New York Times*, November 25, 1994, p. A14.

9. Stanley Meisler, "Madeleine Albright: Representing the United States as World Looks to the United Nations," *Los Angeles Times*, May 2, 1993, p. M3.

Chapter 6. First Year

1. Madeleine Albright, "Current Status of US Policy on Bosnia, Somalia, and UN Reform," *US Department of State Dispatch*, vol. 4, issue 14, April 5, 1993, p. 210.

2. George J. Church, "Anatomy of a Disaster," *Time*, October 18, 1993, p. 42.

3. Nancy Gibbs, "Voice of America," *Time*, December 16, 1996, p. 33.

4. Elaine Sciolino, "Madeleine Albright's Audition," *The New York Times Magazine*, September 22, 1996, p. 67.

5. Colin L. Powell, with Joseph E. Persico, *My American Journey* (New York: Ballantine Books, 1995), p. 501.

6. Ibid.

7. Nancy Gibbs, "The Many Lives of Madeleine," *Time*, February 17, 1997, p. 56.

8. Lee Michael Katz, "U.N. Ambassador Lives a Tale of Two Cities: Job Has New Status, Influence," *USA Today*, April 8, 1993, p. 6A.

Chapter 7. A Tough-Talking Cowgirl

1. Geraldine Baum, "A Diplomatic Core," *Los Angeles Times*, February 8, 1995, p. F11.

2. Jacob Heilbrunn, "Albright's Mission," *The New Republic*, August 22 and 29, 1994, p. 26.

3. Ibid.

4. Elaine Sciolino, "Madeleine Albright's Audition," *The New York Times Magazine*, September 22, 1996, pp. 86–87.

5. Ibid., p. 87.

6. Julia Reed, "Woman of the World," *Vogue*, September 1997, p. 640.

7. Barbara Crossette, "Albright Makes Her U.N. Post a Focal Point," *The New York Times*, November 25, 1994, p. A14.

8. Ibid., p. A1.

9. Barbara Walters, interview with Madeleine Albright, *The 10 Most Fascinating People of 1997*, ABC-TV, December 2, 1997.

10. Ibid.

11. Cindi Leive, "Why Women's Rights Are Foreign Policy," *Glamour*, October 1995, p. 161.

12. Clara Bingham, "Madam Secretary," *Harper's Bazaar*, August 1997, p. 156.

13. Joe Klein, "Diplomacy Without Tears," *The New Yorker*, October 13, 1997, p. 41.

14. Sciolino, p. 67.

15. Klein, p. 43.

Chapter 8. "Madeleine Albright's Audition"

1. Carol Rosenberg, "'Everybody Loves' Tough Albright," *Miami Herald*, March 22, 1996, p. A1.

2. Ibid.

3. Elaine Sciolino, "Madeleine Albright's Audition," *The New York Times Magazine*, September 22, 1996, p. 66.

4. Ibid., p. 64.

5. Michael Dobbs and John M. Goshko, "Albright's Personal Journey Helped Mold Foreign Policy Beliefs," *The Washington Post*, December 6, 1996, p. A25.

6. Sciolino, p. 63.

7. Rowland Evans and Robert Novak, "Madeleine Albright Standing for Freedom," *Reader's Digest*, September 1997, p. 107.

8. Dobbs and Goshko, p. A25.

9. Terry Atlas, "UN Envoy Made Her Mark with a Blunt Style," *Chicago Tribune*, December 6, 1996, sec. 1, p. 1.

10. Barbara Walters, interview with Madeleine Albright, *The 10 Most Fascinating People of 1997*, ABC-TV, December 2, 1997.

11. Ibid.

12. Thomas W. Lippman, "At Albright's Confirmation Hearing, Differences Are Smoothed Over," *The Washington Post*, January 9, 1997, p. A10.

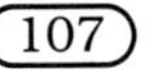

13. Steven Thomma, "Madeleine Albright Speaks of Aggressive Foreign Policy, Strong Human Rights During Her Senate Confirmation Hearings," *Knight-Ridder/Tribune News Service*, January 8, 1997, p. 108K1687.

14. Nancy Gibbs, "The Many Lives of Madeleine," *Time*, February 17, 1997, p. 61.

15. Madeleine Albright, "'We Must Be Forward-looking . . .'" *The Washington Post*, December 6, 1996, p. A25.

16. Harcourt Brace School Publishers, "Madeleine Albright: First Woman to Take Office of Secretary of State," *News Break* <http://www.harcourtschool.com/newsbreak/albright.html> (January 12, 1998).

Chapter 9. The Mystery of Albright's Past

1. Office of the Spokesman of the U.S. Department of State, "Secretary of State Madeleine K. Albright," *Madeleine Albright Remarks to Department of State Employees*, January 27, 1997, <http://secretary.state.gov/www/statements/970127.html> (August 26, 1998).

2. Ibid.

3. Ibid.

4. Ann Blackman, *Seasons of Her Life* (New York: Scribner, 1998), p. 279.

5. Lally Weymouth, "'As I Find Out More, I'm Very Proud': An Exclusive Interview with Madeleine Albright," *Newsweek*, February 24, 1997, p. 30.

6. Ibid., p. 31.

7. Mary Rourke, "Uncovering a Hidden Heritage," *Los Angeles Times*, February 7, 1997, p. E1.

8. Weymouth, p. 31.

9. Michael Dobbs, "Albright Reshapes Role of Nation's Top Diplomat: First Woman in Job Is Forging New Links With Public, Congress," *The Washington Post*, June 15, 1997, p. G12.

10. Fred Coleman, "Small Touches and Big Plans," *U.S. News & World Report*, March 3, 1997, p. 9.

11. Mary Margaret Valenti, "What My Father Taught Me," *McCall's*, July 1998, p. 116.

12. Douglas Waller, "The Albright Touch," *Time*, June 16, 1997, p. 56.

13. Ibid.

14. R. W. Apple Jr., "Albright Visits a Past She Lost, Then Found and Now Embraces," *The New York Times*, July 14, 1997, pp. A1, A4.

15. Dobbs, p. G12.
16. Ibid.
17. Ed Bradley, interview with Madeleine K. Albright, *Sixty Minutes*, CBS-TV, February 9, 1997.
18. Bill Hewitt, "Madam Secretary," *People*, December 23, 1996, p. 48.

Chapter 10. A Star in the State Department

1. Melinda Liu and Russell Watson, "Measuring Madeleine," *Newsweek*, August 11, 1997, p. 34.
2. Ibid.
3. "A Tough Assignment: Peace," *Time for Kids*, September 12, 1997, p. 3.
4. Melinda Liu and Joseph Contreras, "Playing to the Crowd," *Newsweek*, September 22, 1997, p. 46.
5. "Albright Heads for Gulf States: Iraq Accuses U.S. of Trying to Topple Saddam Hussein," *Cedar Rapids* [Iowa] *Gazette*, November 16, 1997, p. 3A.
6. "Albright Says Iraq Agrees to Let U.S. Inspectors Back: Cites Pledge to Russian But Is Still Wary," *The New York Times*, November 20, 1997, p. A1.
7. Robert A. Rankin, "Town Meeting on Iraq Policy Turns Rowdy, But Both Sides Make Their Points," *Knight-Ridder/Tribune News Service*, February 18, 1998, p. 218K2508.
8. Office of the Spokesman, U.S. Department of State, "Albright interview on ABC-TV *Good Morning America,*" *Secretary of State Madeleine K. Albright*, February 19, 1998, <http://secretary.state.gov/www/statements/1998/980219.html> (August 26, 1998).
9. Office of the Spokesman, U.S. Department of State, "Albright Interview on CNN-TV *Larry King Live,*" *Secretary of State Madeleine K. Albright*, August 20, 1998, <http://secretary.state.gov/www/statements/1998/980820a.html> (August 26, 1998).
10. Madeleine Albright, "'We Will Not Be Intimidated,'" *Newsweek*, August 24, 1998, p. 33.
11. Michael Hirsh, "Albright's Old World Ways," *Newsweek*, March 29, 1999, p. 34.
12. "Madeleine Albright Answers Questions About Her Life, Her Interests, and Her Role as Secretary of State," *Questions to the Secretary*, <http://www.state.gov/www/qanda.html> (August 26, 1998).

Books

Burgan, Michael. *Madeleine Albright.* Brookfield, Conn.: Millbrook Press, 1998.

Byman, Jeremy. *Madame Secretary: Story of Madeleine Albright.* Greensboro, N.C.: Morgan Reynolds, 1997.

Freedman, Suzanne. *Madeleine Albright: She Speaks for America.* Danbury, Conn.: Franklin Watts, 1998.

Howard, Megan. *Madeleine Albright.* Minneapolis: Lerner Publications Company, 1998.

Internet Addresses

The Secretary of State's Web site
<http://secretary.state.gov/index.html>

The United Nations Web site
<http://www.un.org>

Index